THE PRECIOUS GEM COLLECTION
The Abundance of My Heart and Journey of My Soul

The Inspirational Literary Work of
Ajá Marie Grant

First Edition

THE PRECIOUS GEM COLLECTION

COPYRIGHT

Copyright© 2015 by Ajá Marie Grant. All rights reserved. In accordance with the U.S. Copyright Act of 1976, the scanning, uploading and electronic sharing of any part of this book without the permission of the publisher constitute unlawful piracy and theft of the author's intellectual property. If you would like to use any material from the book (other than for review purposes), prior written permission must be obtained by contacting the publisher at Zoesoleil@yahoo.com. Thank you for your support, observation and consideration of the author's rights.

The Precious Gem Collection, 1st Edition: The Abundance of My Heart and Journey of My Soul. Terms of Copyright: NO PART OF THIS WRITING MAY BE REPRODUCED OR TRANSMITTED IN ANY FORM, OR BY ANY MEANS, ELECTRONIC OR MECHANICAL, INCLUDING PHOTOCOYPYING, RECORDING, OR BY ANY INFORMATION STORAGE AND RETRIEVAL SYSTEM-EXCEPT BY A REVIEWER WHO MAY QUOTE BRIEF PASSAGES IN A REVIEW TO BE PRINTED IN A MAGAZINE, NEWSPAPER, OR ON THE WEB WITHOUT WRITTEN PERMISSION FROM THE AUTHOR AND PUBLISHER.

NO INFORMATION OF OR PERTAINING TO THE AUTHOR MAY BE DISCLOSED IN ANY FORM, BY ANY MEANS BY FAMILY MEMBERS, FRIENDS, OR ACQUAINTANCES OF THE AUTHOR TO OUTSIDE SOURCES SUCH AS REPORTERS, MAGAZINES, NEWSPAPERS, OR THE GENERAL PUBLIC FOR PERSONAL GAIN WITHOUT PERMISSION FROM THE AUTHOR.

DISCLAIMER: THE OPINIONS EXPRESSED IN THIS BOOK ARE SOLELY THOSE OF Ajá Marie Grant, A LIFE COACH CERTIFIED BY THE LIFE COACH INSTITTUTE OF ORANGE COUNTY, WHO DOES NOT DISPENSE MEDICAL ADVICE, AND IS NOT ACTING IN THE CAPACITY OF A LICENSED PSYCHIATRIST, PSYCHOLOGIST OR OTHER LICENSED OR REGISTERED PROFESSIONAL. THE INFORMATION PRESENTED IN THIS BOOK SHOULD NOT BE TAKEN AS ADVICE THAT IS MEANT TO REPLACE MEDICAL TREATMENT BY A LICENSED HEALTH-CARE PRACTITIONER. ALTHOUGH THE AUTHOR AND PUBLISHER HAVE MADE EVERY ATTEMPT AND EFFORT TO ENSURE THE ACCURACY AND COMPLETENESS OF INFORMATION CONTAINED IN THIS BOOK, WE ASSUME NO RESPONSIBILITY FOR ERRORS, INACCURACIES, OMISSIONS, OR ANY INCONSISTENCY HEREIN. ANY SLIGHTS OF PEOPLE, PLACES, OR ORGANIZATIONS ARE UNINTENTIONAL. USE OF ANY INFORMATION IN THIS BOOK IS AT THE READER'S OWN DISCRETION AND RISK. THE *AUTHOR* AND *ZOE SOLEIL* HEREBY DISCLAIM *ANY* AND *ALL* LIABILITY RESULTING FROM DAMAGE CAUSED BY FOLLOWING ANY RECOMMENDATIONS CONTAINED IN THIS BOOK.

Library of Congress Cataloging-in-Publication Data
Grant, Ajá Marie, 1981-
The precious gem collection: the abundance of my heart and journey of my soul/ Ajá Marie Grant- 1st Edition: New York
ISBN -13: 978-0692504727 (Zoe Soleil, LLC)
ISBN-10: 0692504729

Printed and bound in the United States of America. All rights reserved, including the right of reproduction in whole or in part in any form.

THE PRECIOUS GEM COLLECTION

DEDICATION

This book is dedicated to love and light, and all who seek to emerge, evolve, transform and transcend the ills of this world by serving and elevating humanity.

You walked softly into my life like a whisper in a dream. You enabled me to transcend my history and walk towards destiny. You smiled on me as the light from above illuminated our paths. Our divine encounter caught me by surprise, and the beauty of your soul left me mesmerized. Our spirits intertwined the very first time we locked eyes. Our souls did a dance, it was a two-step met by chance. It was sheer happenstance met by time, space, and divine circumstance. You captured my heart. You captivated my soul. You have elevated me to heights unknown.

You are LOVE…

In Loving Memory of Ida V. Grant, Fannie Mae Pilgrim, Michael Grant, Ruth Lewis and Jonathan Michael Lewis.
- Rest In Peace

THE PRECIOUS GEM COLLECTION

CONTENTS

Preface   8
Introduction-Ajá   9
Defining Moments   10
Acknowledgements   16
Precious Gem Welcome Letter!   19
Poem-Beautiful You Are   21
Angels   22
What Love Is...   23
Divine Vision   24

Chapter 1: EMERGE   26

- Holding Hands
- Come Forth Like Gold
- Count Your Blessings
- Forgiveness
- Friend or Foe? Love Them Both
- Growth
- USC
- Journey to the "City of Angels"
- Leaving The Baggage Behind
- Love & Happiness
- The Greatest Medicine...
- Eyes
- Life Journey
- Live In The Moment
- Nurture Your Nature
- On Top Of The World
- One Day At A Time
- Pamper Thyself!
- Power & Strength
- Promises
- Restoration
- Ride The Wave

Emerge. Evolve. Transform. Transcend.

THE PRECIOUS GEM COLLECTION

Chapter 2: EVOLVE   56

- Seasons Change
- Speak Life To It!
- Strides In The Right Direction
- Sunshine After The Rain
- Beautiful Essence
- Commit Thy Work
- Fear
- God Has Not Forgotten
- The Power of Prayer
- Love It, Leave It, Let It Go
- Make Room For Love
- New Beginnings
- Put On The Right Hat!
- Restore Your Soul
- The Choice Is Yours
- The Storms of Life
- Wonderfully Made
- Food For Thought***Renew Your Mind
- Give It To God
- Rare & Precious Jewels
- What Dreams Are Made Of
- Come In Out Of The Rain

Chapter 3: TRANSFORM   91

- Forget The Past
- Get Up! Get Out! Do Something!
- Ignite The Fire Within
- Peace Be Still!
- Redemption Through Christ
- When You've Done All You Can
- Life Lessons
- Love Thyself!
- Heal Thyself!
- Learn To Say No!

THE PRECIOUS GEM COLLECTION

- The Power Of Focus
- Let Peace Be Your Anchor
- Transformation
- All Things Work Together For Good
- Do What You Love
- Gratitude &Praise
- Worthy Of All Things Good
- Self-Acceptance
- What Moves You?
- Burdens
- I Am Found
- A New Day!

Chapter 4: TRANSCEND   122

- Assurance
- Define Who You are
- Choices
- Change Of Heart
- That Special Someone
- The Seat Of Consciousness
- Time
- Victorious
- Wait On The Lord!
- Intuition
- Serendipity
- Miscommunication
- Butterflies
- If The Gift Is Still Good
- Fall In Love With Your Life
- Manifest The Greatness Within
- We're All In Need Of Love
- Short & Sweet
- Exhortation
- Impressions
- Let The Silence Be Broken

THE PRECIOUS GEM COLLECTION

- To Be A Kid Again

Chapter 5: SOAR   142

- Spread Your Wings & Fly
- Stay Fly...Live Life!
- What Is Your Mission Statement?
- Canvas Of Life
- Window To Your Soul
- The Gift Of Solitude
- Pain Is A Gift
- One Wish
- Ten Hut!
- Dynamite
- Enlarge Your Vision
- Scars
- Sacrifice
- Redefine Who You Are
- Happiness
- Perseverance
- What Is A Hater Really?
- Truth
- A Mother's Love
- Seize the Day!
- Daddy's Little Girl
- Live

Go To Your Destiny!   191
One Chapter Ends...Precious Gem Tribute   193
A Prayer For You   195
Celebrate Life*   196
A Special Invitation   197
About The Author   198
Contact   200

Emerge. Evolve. Transform. Transcend.

THE PRECIOUS GEM COLLECTION

PREFACE

The Precious Gem Collection: The Abundance of My Heart and Journey of My Soul is a compilation of inspirational pieces that are based on my life's journey. All of the inspirations in this edition are composed of insights that promote empowerment, enrichment, self-discovery, growth, healing, wellness, and enlightenment. They are written from a personal perspective, one that holds humankind in consciousness. Dealing with contemporary issues and providing insights that will assist anyone who endeavors to embark on their own journey of growth and self-discovery, each piece seeks to inform, empower, and inspire.

Holding firmly to the belief that any gift that is God given should be freely shared, as the true blessing resides in the giving, it is my hope that the baton will be passed and in turn cause a snowball effect and spark a revolution. My purpose and mission statement not only speaks to the heart of those who seek to change their lives, but also those who seek to affect change in the lives of others. In addition, I believe that this work will serve as a ladder of enlightenment for those who are looking to accelerate humanity. I believe that this endeavor will not only serve as a vital catalyst in the lives and communities of many, but also as a vehicle towards forward progression. Let's break the cycles that keep us fettered by restraints. It's time we started improving upon and stepping out of the conditions that try so hard to beset us. We do not have to be bound by the ills of this world. We can live a life uninhibited by traditions or that which seeks to impede upon our growth and forward progression. It is time to rid our lives of that which no longer serves us, such entities that seek to stifle our growth. The sky truly is the limit Precious Gems. Let us work to continually walk in humility and serve humankind. Let us put our energy towards accelerating humanity. The world is your stage Precious Gems, light it up!

THE PRECIOUS GEM COLLECTION

Ajá

Ajá is a genuine force to reckon with, a woman whose soul and character is reflected in every movement, as she seeks to inspire on many levels. Her vision is as clear as it is golden. A vision that will take her far beyond what is current, and into a realm that is everlasting. She speaks a universal language of love that is understood, and felt by humankind. A language that speaks to the heart and soul of every individual she encounters. She is adorned with wisdom, a crown of grace and beauty that is God given. Her feet are firmly planted in love. Her eyes are the window to her soul. Her strength is inexhaustible, as it derives from an omnipotent source. Her style is unique. She combines talent, creativity, and ingenuity, as she paints a beautiful mosaic with her heart for the entire world to see. She will touch your heart with the stroke of a pen, and win your soul with truth. You will be captivated by every note that she sings, as her heart plays a tune that can only be felt by the soul. The brightest light illuminates her path. She dwells in harmony, coexisting as an unlimited life form. Her spirit is as free as a butterfly as she soars on the wings of faith, unencumbered by the pangs of life. The sound of her voice is as sweet as the melody a hummingbird sings. She knows no limits. She is boundless in her efforts. Abounding in love, she has a heart of gold. A rare and precious jewel is she.

Ajá, a name that speaks for itself....

THE PRECIOUS GEM COLLECTION

DEFINING MOMENTS

Throughout my life, leadership has taken on many different forms and meanings, as my understanding and beliefs about leadership have evolved and transformed through a wide variety of experiences.

When I think of leadership, the first thing that comes to my mind is "Lead by example," something that was instilled in me from childhood by my parents. The definition of leadership to me is the act of guiding or directing an individual(s) and/or a group towards fulfilling a common goal. It often means turning a single effort into a joint and collective effort, as one's vision cannot and will not remain singular if it is to come to fruition. It means motivating, inspiring, and pushing people to utilize their full potential to obtain desired end results, while striving for excellence in the process.

To lead others to achieve greatness on any level, one must first walk in that greatness, and most often it does not happen overnight. It takes preparation and much discipline, as the pruning and development of one's character is a tedious and sometimes gruesome process. This undertaking is not even something that we as individuals can even put a time limit on, nor it is something that we often have control of, as life is made up of a series of events that involve people, places and things that all play a huge part in who we will in essence become. In addition, the journey to "becoming" is not always laced with ribbons and roses, as it is usually the hard places, the very valleys of life that tend to shape a person's entire being.

Leadership involves many critical factors, and the beautiful part about it is that these factors are different for each and every individual across the board. And, while you may find a few similarities from one individual to the next, I'm sure you will find many more distinctions as every individual's definition of leadership will be unique to their own experiences.

THE PRECIOUS GEM COLLECTION

It's sort of like a fingerprint or snowflake, you will never encounter the same ones, as each of them are unique by nature. For me personally, leadership involves having a keen vision, sharp focus, determination, drive and ambition, patience, perseverance, endurance, resilience, flexibility, wisdom and counsel, goal-setting and delegation/relegation, organization and time-management, and laughter.

If one has a keen vision, that means that come hell or high water, that vision will remain rooted and in place, even if the cast and characters change, give up, delay, rebel, and forfeit the vision. If you as the leader remain steadfast and unmovable, always abounding in your life's work, there's a great chance that you will see your vision come to pass.

If one has a sharp focus, that means that no matter what is going on around you, be it peaceful demonstrations in support of your vision, or fierce and reckless opposition, your focus will not be shaken and you will keep the main thing as the main thing. Of course life throws curveballs, and of course we get discouraged along the way, but there comes a time when one must put on blinders like a horse, neither looking to the left or to the right and stay focused on the path that is set before them. The race is not always given to the swift, sometimes slow and steady does win the race.

Determination will take you a long way as a leader, for whom or what can stop and unbridled and determined soul? Not much or many I presume. If every time you fall, you get back up and go at it again and again, eventually you will meet the mark.

Endurance and perseverance go hand-in-hand in my opinion, as you cannot have one without the other. It is very difficult to endure under the extreme pressures of life, and the wear and tear that long-suffering imposes on your mind, body and soul can be unbearable at times. However, this is where perseverance comes into play. Tenacity goes a mighty long way. It's just like water against a large and firmly grounded rock, it may take some time, but eventually the rock will give way and be moved by the persistence of the water.

THE PRECIOUS GEM COLLECTION

Drive and ambition are close cousins as well, for that innate pull driving you towards that vision will be a catalyst for you as a leader to make it to the finish line, and the strong desire wrapped up as ambition is what's necessary to push you towards the goal.

Patience is necessary (especially as a leader), for you will be stretched beyond your means at times and the capacity to tolerate trouble, delay, suffering, indifference, the idiosyncrasies of others, and life's nuances period, one must employ patience. Resilience is where the rubber meets the road, for it is the hard places that have the potential to break a person. However, even the "breaking" can be used to one's advantage, as the being that emerges from the wreckage has the capacity to evolve into a new and improved version of the being that once was. The human spirit is hard to break.

Flexibility is another factor essential to leadership, as things change and we as people change. One must have the ability to roll with the punches and flow with every curve, as life does not go in a straight line, never has and it never will. You must be able to yield to different influences and opinions, but only if they are helping the vision and not a detriment to the vision. You must be able to adapt to the "new" that may emerge, especially as it concerns people, places and things that may enhance the vision.

Wisdom and counsel are key elements to succeeding as a leader, as the marriage between your own wisdom and the wisdom of others that have either gone before you or who are standing with you will be pertinent to your survival, as well as the survival of the group that you're leading. Counsel is important especially as it concerns decision-making, for I believe that in the multitude of counselors there is much success (but I do also believe that there are times when must go at it alone and follow their gut).

Goal-setting and delegation/relegation are very important, as goals are key to fulfilling the vision one step at a time. One must be able to delegate and distribute tasks and responsibilities, as well as relegate and step down so to say in an effort to gain understanding, and in order for

THE PRECIOUS GEM COLLECTION

goals to be met in an efficient and timely fashion. This brings me back to leading by example, as a leader may sometimes have to do the very thing he is leading others to do to not only gain the respect of the group, but to also be able to understand the group's stance as a group.

Organization and time-management go hand-in-hand as well, as deadlines have to be met and in order for deadlines to be met, things must be organized in a manner where we are able to meet deadlines and not miss deadline. Time is of the essence, and it truly does not wait for anyone. It is important to manage time wisely as a leader, as well as to set the proper tone for those who you are leading.

And last but not least, it may sound strange to some, but laughter for me has always been one of the most significant and critical factors of leadership. I do not know where I would be without laughter, for it truly does cure the maladies of the heart, just as it has the power to heal and uplift the soul. Laughter is medicine and I am a firm believer that laughter soothes the heaviness that can sometimes surround one's life. The aforementioned thoughts relate to my defining moment and the event(s) that shaped me into the person I am today in a very big way, as most of my experiences either as a leader, or as one being led all revolve around this defining moment.

Life has been one of my greatest teachers, as my defining moment occurred at the age of eighteen when I ventured off to Los Angeles, California to contend for my dream of becoming a writer and life coach. On May 1, 2000 I left behind family, friends, and the comforts of home to gain some real world experience while pursuing my Bachelor's Degree in Creative Writing at the University of Southern California. However, much to my surprise, the journey unfolded much differently than I expected, for having come from a nurturing and protective environment, I must admit that it was not an easy transition, and it actually turned out to be more of a walk of faith. I eventually welcomed the challenge as I embarked on a journey of self-discovery, as it is in Los Angeles, the "City of Angels" where I learned a great deal about endurance and perseverance.

THE PRECIOUS GEM COLLECTION

On June 18th, 2001, the morning of my nineteenth birthday, I received the devastating news of my Grandmother's passing. This crisis deeply impacted my life and transformed me significantly through the shaping of my character. Additionally, it placed a profound new perspective on my entire life, as the sudden and unexpected death of my best friend caused me to reevaluate my life and paint a whole new picture on the canvas of life. I was at a standstill. There I stood, I had made the transition from adolescence to adulthood, but all that I knew to be solid was suddenly shaken. My faith, my dream, and my hope were all put to the test, and I believe this is where the classroom of life really got my attention. After my rude awakening, I realized that I had a decision to make: I had to choose between everything I worked for in California and moving back to New York City to start all over. I was at a crossroads in my life, I lived in Los Angeles for two years, working full-time at the University of Southern California and attending school full-time in the evening. I did not want to give up the life I made for myself in sunny Southern California, but deep in my heart I knew that it was time to return to the drawing board.

I went through a very gruesome mourning process, and it was very difficult for me to move from that place in my life. However, I needed healing to fill the huge void in my heart. Making the transition from one place in your life into the next can be very challenging; however the positive results that transpire from those challenges are priceless.

I decided to move back to New York City on April 1, 2002, and what seemed like a difficult and daunting task, quickly became simple as I began to lay the foundation for my future. Returning home was deeper than just communing with family and old friends, it was about overcoming a great challenge. I found comfort amongst family and friends, and that enabled me to find peace with the loss of my grandmother. During the time that I took off from school, I ventured into the working world to further pursue professional endeavors. In addition, not only did I grow professionally, but I was able to grow personally as well. I was able to gain the knowledge and tools necessary for me to succeed not only in the working world, but in the world at large. My professional experience afforded me the ability to cultivate my interests, exercise my skills, meet a wide array of people, and travel to places I've only dreamed of.

THE PRECIOUS GEM COLLECTION

I also found that the place where I began was exactly where I needed to be in order to begin again. For the past decade I've used my life experiences (much of which was birthed out of my experiences in Los Angeles) as a means to communicate and deal effectively with a very diverse audience. I gave up everything that I had obtained in Los Angeles, and I regained the strength to recapture my dream with a renewed focus, greater courage, and newfound determination and inspiration. Life grants an inexplicable amount of strength and courage. You never know just how far you can fly unless you try. If you can close your eyes, open your heart, and see life beyond the horizon, then you open yourself up to unlimited possibilities.

In this race we call life, we are often in a hurry to reach a certain destiny, but we must realize that the race is not given to the swift or to the strong, but to the one who endures to the end. So I say again, life has been one of my greatest teachers, and I look forward to a lifetime of learning and exploration. Moving forward, I expect to obtain invaluable experience and the marketable skills necessary to pursue my life work in an environment that will assist me in cultivating my ideas, and make available the necessary resources that will provide for professional achievement and personal growth.

THE PRECIOUS GEM COLLECTION

ACKNOWLEDGEMENTS

Lord,
I owe it all to you, and so I give it back! Thank You for Your everlasting love. Your grace is sufficient, and Your mercy endures forever. You set me high upon a rock, and You never let my foot slip. You always catch me when I fall. You never slumber, nor do You sleep. I AM who I AM because of You. My heart, my mind, my body, and my soul belong to You. This fact remains the same, and forever and always will be true. With my whole heart, I love You and I serve You. My life belongs to You. I give You all the Glory and Honor. You have given me a Secret Place where I find rest, peace, and restoration for my soul. There is love and protection in Your sanctuary. Continue to guide me, mold me, and use me Lord. Loving you endlessly every day that I live, breathe, and have my being.

"My soul finds rest in God alone; He alone is my rock and my salvation, he is my fortress, I will never be shaken." (Psalms 62:56)

Mom & Dad,
Where would I be without you? I am an extension of you, a reflection of all the love and beauty you possess inside. You have shown me the way, and you never allowed me to stray too far away from the path that was set before me. In good times and in bad, you have been my safe haven, my comfort zone, and most importantly my shelter from the storm. Aside from being two of the greatest parents in the whole wide world, you are two of the most beautiful and benevolent individuals I have ever had the pleasure of knowing and loving. I extend not only my heartfelt gratitude, but also my love and sincere appreciation for you both. My love for you is endless.

Matthew Vincent, My Precious Son...
You are the very beat of my heart! God gave me the world when He gave me you, and so every single day I vow to give the world to you. My life was completely transformed by your conception, it evolved upon your entrance, and every moment I am falling higher and higher. You are my precious seed, and I love you with every breath that I breathe.

THE PRECIOUS GEM COLLECTION

My Precious Siblings,
My darling sisters, and my dear brother, we have walked this journey of life collectively and separately at times. However, love always brings us back to the place where we belong. May the love that keeps us together, always keep us from drifting apart. I love you endlessly.

Erica Charlene Banks,
You are my twin soul. A sister and a friend you have been, one who has consistently held my hand through life's peaks and valleys, as you have shown me what true and unwavering friendship resembles. Let's share our hearts, goals and dreams for eternity. Words cannot express the magnitude of my gratitude and appreciation for you. I love you E.

Kareem & Roxy,
You are a real life dream team fashioned by God. You have been more than friends; you are family, as your family has become my family over the years. You have watched over me and helped me grow. You have been there for me through some of my best, and some of my darkest times. I love you.

Raymie,
You have always been consistent, down with A from day one. You never cease to amaze me. You have held Big A down throughout adolescence, and all the way up and through adulthood. You are a rare one and a real one, and I love you for life. You were strategically placed in my life at the divine and appointed time. Thank you for being true to yourself, true to the game, and true to my name. Don't ever change. *Loyalty is everything.*

Twin Flame,
Our connection transcends space and time. We dwell in our very own galaxy, a world that is all our own. Our friendship is a beautiful fusion of hearts and souls combined, as our lives are clustered together like stars carefully placed and woven together by gravitational magnetism. You are my best friend and confidante, and the journey would not be complete without you. It's been one heck of a ride, and through every dip and curve you have stood by my side. The world is our stage, so let's light it up throughout eternity! I love you to infinity and beyond...

THE PRECIOUS GEM COLLECTION

480 & Its Constituents,
You have all played a special part in my personal growth and the development of my character. Thank you for your love and support.

Precious Gems,
I want to take the time to extend my gratitude and appreciation to the much cherished Gems in my life. I have had the pleasure and honor of encountering and entertaining some extraordinary men and women throughout my life; some of whom have passed on leaving behind their legacy as they left their imprint on the world, and others who have passed the baton to me, whom I have formed friendships with that have flourished over the years. There are also some new budding friendships whose seeds have been watered and are blossoming as we speak. I thank God for gracing my life with your presence Precious Gems, and for allowing His love to come forth through each and every single one of you. Without you all, there would be no inspiration. You have given me a reason to strive and do all the things that God purposed in me to do. You have shown me that with a willing spirit and an open heart, you can do anything!

Thank you for shining your light in my life, and for allowing me to shine my light in yours. Thank you for the pearls of wisdom that you have bestowed upon me on this journey. Thank you for leading by example. Thank you for your truth and dexterity. Thank you for the experiences we have shared, all of the laughter, joy, and tears. Most of all, thank you for your love, support, inspiration, and prayers over the years. You are loved.

As you journey through life, you will form certain bonds; and those connections will open you up to unique experiences. These distinct opportunities will play a major part in your personal growth and professional development, and if one is fortunate, these bonds will last a lifetime...

To all who have played an integral part in the story of my life, I thank you from the bottom of my heart to the top of my soul. To my West coast kings and queens, my East coast queens and kings, my comrades up North, and mi familia down South, you know who you are. I love you.

Emerge. Evolve. Transform. Transcend.

THE PRECIOUS GEM COLLECTION

Dear Precious Gems,

It is the eve of a new beginning. I am standing on the threshold of tomorrow and my path is illuminated with light. My focus is clear, and as I tread through each new day, I vow to embrace every precious moment and celebrate life.

As I welcome you on this everlasting journey of inspiration, I want to take the time to thank you for accompanying me on this road. As you walk down this path of life, and tread upon this journey of inspiration, may the road curve to meet your every expectation.

God has blessed me with an opportunity to be used as an instrument to convey messages of love and inspiration. May this instrument not only be used to play a fine tune that will touch your heart, but also bless your soul. The opportunity that I have been granted to share my life experiences, lessons learned, hopes, and dreams with you is a much cherished gift. These inspirations truly are the compilation and abundance of my heart and journey of my soul.

As I sit and ponder my heartfelt expressions, I can't help but to give God the glory as it is He Who speaks through the waterfalls of my heart. As they flow, and overflow into the hearts and minds of every individual who seeks inspiration, my hope is not only that every word comes to life as you read them, but that you allow them to take residence in your hearts and minds, as they empower you to transform your soul and change your life. May these words from my heart to yours provide sustenance and warmth in a world that can sometimes be cold. In a world so full of complexities, finding oneself may be one of the toughest challenges yet. However, with the support, love, and assistance of the universe, and all of its constituents, we as human beings are enabled to individually and collectively unveil every spectacular part of who we are as we embark on our own journey of self-discovery and personal growth.

THE PRECIOUS GEM COLLECTION

      We are all like butterflies in the garden of life, fluttering to life's fine tune. Alight upon the soul of another and let your light so shine before men, that they may see your good works, and glorify your Father which is in heaven.

      May you be inspired this day, and uplifted upon every word you read. From my mouth to God's ears, I wish for every soul to find its place, every heart to beat with love, every light to be met with the light from above, every tear of sorrow to be replaced with shouts of joy, every dream deferred to be fulfilled, and for everyone to see the good in every individual that they meet. I cherish you Precious Gems, as you have been added to my special treasure chest of inspiration.

Love & Light,
~Ajá

THE PRECIOUS GEM COLLECTION

BEAUTIFUL YOU ARE

Men and Women, let us unite. Let us stand together as one. Let us put aside every worldly ill that tries so hard to beset us. Anything that goes contrary to what God intended for us to be must cease. Don't you know who you are? You are beautiful and powerful beyond measure indeed! There is no room for negativity, jealousy, gluttony, or deceit. Let us promote love, truth, respect and peace, for beautiful you are, and beautiful you will always be...

Beautiful you are
Made in the image and likeness of God
Your eyes, the window to your soul
Your heart, a reflection of God's love
Your smile, a light from above
Your soul, a precious gift to behold

Love hard!
Stand strong!
You are society's backbone
Strength, Courage, and Wisdom is your crown

Fearless. Strong. Uninhibited.
Take your place
Stand your ground
Men and Women, beautiful you are
And beautiful you will always be!

THE PRECIOUS GEM COLLECTION

ANGELS

*"And the angel answering said unto him,
I am Gabriel that stands in the presence of God;
And I was sent to speak unto thee,
And to bring these good tidings."
~Luke 1:19 (NIV)*

Angels are ministering spirits sent to those who will inherit salvation. Have you been sent an angel? I can honestly say I have on numerous occasions. How has this affected you? I was encouraged, but often found myself repeating the same negative behaviors. Why have I struggled so much? To learn obedience! I've learned that you can't harbor hate and know love at the same time. Confusion is many opposing thoughts running rampant in the mind. What you concentrate on will surely manifest itself one way or another, for as a man thinketh so shall he be. Just imagine what would happen if we concentrated on eliminating the world's ills collectively. What a world it would be! Experiment with your thoughts and operate at the highest level of your thinking.

*"For He shall give His angels charge over you,
to keep you in all your ways.
In their hands, they shall bear you up.
Lest you dash your foot against a stone."
~Psalm 91: 11& 12 (NIV)*

May your winding path be crossed by a wise one, and may your spirits perceive recognition.

*"Be careful to entertain strangers, for you never know if you may have unwittingly entertained and angel."
~Hebrews 13:2 (NIV)*

~VPG

Emerge. Evolve. Transform. Transcend.

THE PRECIOUS GEM COLLECTION

WHAT LOVE IS...

"If I speak in the tongues of men and of angels, but have not love, I am only a resounding gong or a clanging cymbal. If I have the gift of prophecy and can fathom all mysteries and all knowledge, and if I have a faith that can move mountains, but have not love, I am nothing. If I give all I possess to the poor and surrender my body to the flames, but have not love, I gain nothing. Love is patient, love is kind. It does not envy, it does not boast, it is not proud. It is not rude, it is not self-seeking, it is not easily angered, it keeps no record of wrongs. Love does not delight in evil but rejoices with the truth. It always protects, always trusts, always hopes, always perseveres. Love never fails. But where there are prophecies, they will cease; where there are tongues, they will be stilled; where there is knowledge, it will pass away. For we know in part and we prophesy in part, but when perfection comes, the imperfect disappears. When I was a child, I talked like a child, I thought like a child, I reasoned like a child. When I became a man, I put childish ways behind me. Now we see but a poor reflection as in a mirror; then we shall see face to face. Now I know in part; then I shall know fully, even as I am fully known. And now these three remain: faith, hope and love. But the greatest of these is love."

~*1Corinthians 13:1-13(NIV)*

THE PRECIOUS GEM COLLECTION

DIVINE VISION

"For the vision is yet for an appointed time, but at the end it shall speak, and not lie: though it tarry, wait for it; because it will surely come, it will not tarry."
~Habakkuk 2:3 (NIV)

Emerge. Evolve. Transform. Transcend.

THE PRECIOUS GEM COLLECTION
The Abundance of My Heart and Journey of My Soul

Ajá Marie Grant

THE PRECIOUS GEM COLLECTION

CHAPTER 1

***

EMERGE

Emerge. Evolve. Transform. Transcend.

THE PRECIOUS GEM COLLECTION

HOLD MY HAND

Walk with me, talk with me, cry with me, laugh with me… I am holding your hand! On this journey, I have crossed paths with a multitude of beautiful souls, and one cannot help but to believe that love can reign in a world that can be so cold. As I welcome you all on this everlasting journey of inspiration, I want to take the time to thank you Precious Gems for accompanying me on this road. Many people walk in and out of our lives, and some leave footprints in our hearts, allowing us to never forget that we are loved and extremely special. You will receive kindness from strangers along the way, and you must always be careful to entertain strangers, for you never know when you may have unknowingly entertained an angel. Yes, there will be ups and downs on this journey. However, we have the ability to turn our trials into treasure and our mess into a message by focusing on the positive that comes from our tribulation. We never know where the road will lead us, all we can do is move forward and trust that God will light our path. While we are here on this earth, we have to make the best of every day. We must cherish the good times, and reflect on the good days when we are struck with bad days. Life is not always easy, but we will make it through if we hold on when times get rough. When the road gets a little bumpy, put on your brakes and take your time. Don't stop going. Keep moving forward, the road will get a little smoother as you go along. Watch. Rest. Listen. There will be signs along the way that will guide you and give you clear direction. Allow God to sit in the driver's seat and direct your path. You will reach your destination in peace…

THE PRECIOUS GEM COLLECTION

COME FORTH LIKE GOLD

Has there ever been a time in your life when it seemed like chaos surrounded you, and that hardship was on every hand? Has there ever been a time when it seemed like no one could possibly understand what you were going through, and no matter how many people were in your camp, you still felt alone in the wilderness? Well Precious Gems, I am here to tell you that even in the midst of the wilderness, you are not walking alone.

In the wilderness, character and strength are built. In the wilderness, you will be tried and tested, and there will be times when you feel forsaken. In the wilderness, people may turn their backs on you. In the wilderness, faith is fueled, love speaks and hope emerges. In the wilderness, you will find peace. In the wilderness, you are fine-tuned and refined. In the wilderness, you find out who you really are. In the wilderness, you find out who your friends are. In the wilderness, fear may arise, but courage creeps up to sustain you. In the wilderness, you find that there is strength in your struggle. In the wilderness, you are forced to shut your physical eye and trust the spirit within. It the wilderness, your inner voice begins to speak louder, and it overpowers the negative voice of others. In the wilderness, it gets darker before the dawn. In the wilderness, you are being taught life lessons. In the wilderness, nature becomes your best friend. In the wilderness, your pillow may be drenched with tears day in and day out. In the wilderness, you are forced to grow in the right direction. In the wilderness, you are forced to let go of the old. In the wilderness, you are cleansed within, and after your wilderness experience is over, you will come forth as gold...

We have all faced, or may someday have to face wilderness experiences, but the end result is gold. So even when you are in the wilderness, always remember that you are going *through* and that God will bring you out.

THE PRECIOUS GEM COLLECTION

There is a blessing in store for you when you come out of the wilderness, just go through. You are coming out as GOLD!

THE PRECIOUS GEM COLLECTION

COUNT YOUR BLESSINGS

So often we spend more time focusing on what we do not have, instead of really acknowledging what we do have. I am sure that there are a few things that we would all like to aspire to, obtain, or achieve. However, we must be grateful for what we already possess, and where we have made it thus far. I know that life can sometimes be a struggle, and that there are some folks who have a little more or less than others, but we must learn to be content in every situation. If we are not content with little, how on earth are we going to be content with much? What I have learned in my years spent on this earth, is that God will take you farther than any amount of money ever could, and joy will add to your life in so many beautiful ways. You would be surprised how many people on this earth have tons of money in their bank accounts. However, they can hardly enjoy it. You would be surprised how many people live in the nicest houses, but they will never be able to make their house a home because they are miserable. You would be surprised how many people drive the nicest cars, but will most often be the only one riding in them. Without joy, peace, or love within, how can one fully enjoy anything? Having much and doing the most does not have to consist of driving the hottest car, living in the nicest house, or having tons of money in a bank account. You are doing the most, and you are blessed with much if you have a family that loves and supports you. You are blessed if you have friends that simply adore you. You are blessed if you have a job that brings you joy and pays your bills. You are blessed if you have a roof over your head and food on your table. You are blessed if your limbs are intact, and your senses are working, and you have a clean bill of health. Most importantly, you are blessed if you have breath of life and awaken each day to see a new day. I know that we live in a world where the finer things in life are desired and warranted, but are you any less of a person if you do not possess it all?

THE PRECIOUS GEM COLLECTION

Not at all! The more we focus on what we have, we are blessed with more than we could possibly imagine. When we count our blessings, we subtract our burdens, and we make room for more joy, more peace, and more love to reign. The finer things in life will simply be a beautiful addition, an enhancement and an extra added bonus to your prosperous and purpose-filled existence.

THE PRECIOUS GEM COLLECTION

FORGIVENESS

In life, people will hurt you and do you wrong, but it is how you respond and handle them that most often determine the outcome. It is not always easy to be the bigger person when someone has intentionally wronged you, and when all you want to do is take matters into your own hands. However, for the benefit of all parties involved, one is better off walking away and leaving it in God's hands. People reap what they sow, and it is not up to us to determine the punishment for their actions. Even if you do respond in the same manner in which you were treated, that does not solve anything because two wrongs do not make a right. I am here to tell you that killing someone with kindness is the best thing that you could do, because while you may be hurt and trying to figure out why someone would intentionally bring you pain, you must remember that misery loves company. When someone is hurting, sometimes all they can do is focus in on their own pain and place it on someone else. Their intent may not be to do so, but that may be all they know. So often we expect from others what we know we would give of ourselves, but we must realize that everyone is unique in their own way, and we all deal with things differently. So the next time someone does you wrong and you want to take it to the streets, tear them to pieces, and kill them with harmful words, please try your best to extinguish them with love and kindness. By you doing so, they may be convicted to hopefully do what is right as they begin to see the error in their own ways. This will leave your mind, body, and soul at ease, while also leaving you with a clear conscience. Love is the greatest weapon anyone could possess, and if we use it correctly, we would be able to battle and defeat negativity on a grand scale. I am not saying that it will always be easy, but it can't hurt to at least try and take a step in the right direction.

THE PRECIOUS GEM COLLECTION

FRIEND or FOE? * LOVE THEM BOTH!

What do you do when it is no longer just your foes, but instead your "friends" who smile in your face, and all the while they want to take your place? Knowing that they don't even want you in the race and it is you that they want to replace? The answer is that you must shower them with love and kindness, and bless them on their way. People will betray you and try to take your smile, but you have to keep on living and go that extra mile. When the world is on your shoulder and you need a helping hand, you find the world is growing colder and it's hard to understand. You ask yourself, "Why must life be so hard and the problems you can't discard?" The answer lies inside, and that is where you start. Remember that hope lives in you; simply look inside your heart. If God be for you, then who can be against you?

We are human and imperfect, but we serve a mighty God, and in Him we are fearfully and wonderfully made. I will be the first to tell you that it is not always easy to extinguish hate with love, but I find that love is the only way that we can win. We possess a powerful tool Gems, and that tool is love. Love always wins, and love always puts up a good fight. You can bet your bottom dollar that love does reign and will succeed. So don't fret or get discouraged when folk rise up against you, for greater is He who is in you.

"He alone is my rock and my salvation; he is my fortress, I shall never be shaken." (Psalm 62:6-NIV)

You can do all things through Christ which strengthens you! (Philippians 4:13-NIV)

"What shall we then say to these things? If God be for us, who can be against us?" (Romans 8:31-NIV)

THE PRECIOUS GEM COLLECTION

GROWTH

There comes a time in each of our lives when we are summoned to release & let go! Letting go of someone or something is not always easy, but we find that we must release certain things in order to move forward in life. Sometimes we hold onto things because they give us a sense of belonging and comfort. However, those same things that give us comfort are often times the same things that stagnate and disable us. Growth is a huge part of life, and growing is sometimes painful and uncomfortable. However, we must all cast away the old and make room for the new. However, in the process we must be patient with ourselves, for everything under the sun has a season. "There is a time for everything, and a season for every activity under heaven." (Ecclesiastes 3:1) During the growth process, you may sometimes feel like you are being stretched and pulled in a direction that you had not anticipated, but I guarantee you that it is all for your good. Take butterflies for instance, they are some of the most beautiful creatures on this earth, and yet they did not start out as butterflies, they had to transform from caterpillars into butterflies. What we see when we look at a butterfly is the definition and beauty of their wings. However, what we do not often see is their struggle in the process of becoming that beautiful creature. We are all like butterflies in a sense; we have all had to grow into to our own beautiful wings. However, until we spread our wings, we will never know how far we can fly. Don't be afraid to release and let go of the things that may be causing you pain, or that may be a hindrance or stumbling block in your path. There are beautiful things ahead of you, and all you have to do is claim them. Follow your heart and don't be afraid to spread those beautiful wings. In addition, remember to breathe when life gets a little rough. Where there is peace, there is certainty, all you have to do is have faith and keep moving forward.

THE PRECIOUS GEM COLLECTION

Life is full of choices, and choices are not always easy to make. Walk by faith and not by sight. Listen to your heart and let God lead the way. May your path be illuminated by the brightest light and may love, peace, and joy sustain you along the way.

THE PRECIOUS GEM COLLECTION

USC

You raised me. You opened your arms wide and you gave me a place to call home. You fed me, you clothed me, and you gave me my wings. You were my rite of passage, my coming of age. You taught me how to fly, and it is because of you that I sing. You enriched me with your traditions. You gave me experience and you provided sustenance and warmth. Your trees hugged me as they provided shade in the summertime. I never really experienced a true winter, but the rain in February kept me inside. Can we talk about autumn and spring? The rain stained the ground as it fell from above. Leaves danced around the park as they fell from the trees. The water nourished the grass and enabled it to sprout. The flower beds were kissed by the sun after heavy rains, and birds found their nesting place in a place high above ground. The squirrels scurried about in search of their daily bread, and the twigs rested peacefully on the ground awaiting a lighter step. Because of you, I could not help but to reach for the sky. You gave me my wings; you taught me how to fly…

THE PRECIOUS GEM COLLECTION

JOURNEY TO THE "CITY OF ANGELS"

One of the greatest challenges I have ever had to face in my life was the sudden and unexpected death of my grandmother Ida. It took great effort and willingness on my part, to face and overcome this challenge. My grandmother was an extremely prominent figure in my life, being the source of much of my inspiration, strength, support, encouragement, and motivation. She played a significant role in my life since the day I was brought into this world. She was more than just a grandmother; she was my friend and confidante. She was a huge part of every birthday celebration, she was present at every graduation, and she rejoiced in all of my achievements. She believed in me, and she made me feel capable of reaching higher heights. I lived with her in New York City for one year prior to moving to Los Angeles, and during that year our relationship grew tremendously. There was an unbreakable bond that was formed between us, and I could not imagine my life without her.

What started as a mere dream, slowly merged into reality on May 1st, 2000 when I decided to follow my heart and venture out to Los Angeles at the age of eighteen. This trip had been long awaited, as well as a vision that had been kept alive since childhood. This was the beginning of a lifetime experience for me, and it was deemed impossible by the non-dreamers and disbelievers in my circle of family and friends. However, my Grandmother encouraged me to follow my heart and chase my dreams.

In order to begin my journey, I set aside the month of May to find employment and a dwelling place so that I would be situated in time to celebrate my birthday on June 18th, 2000. I stayed in a part of Los Angeles called: Westlake Mac Arthur Park, where I felt as if I was living inside of Pandora's Box. I stayed in the Olympic Hotel on 7th & Alvarado for a couple of weeks just to get my feet planted in Los Angeles; and being a young woman all odds seemed to be against me.

THE PRECIOUS GEM COLLECTION

I started to get discouraged because of my surroundings and the limited amount of time I had to get settled, but something inside of me would not let me give up. I spent many nights praying, and I decided to leave everything in God's hands. There were times when I could have easily given up in the face of adversity, but I stood my ground and beat the odds. Dreams are often hard to follow, but as long as you believe in them and have faith in yourself, there is nothing that you cannot achieve. There I stood, I had made the transition from childhood to adulthood, and I was living my dream to the fullest. I received kindness from strangers along the way, and I had also learned a great deal about endurance and perseverance. I reaped the benefits of all the seeds I have sown.

I lived in Los Angeles for two years, working full-time at the University of Southern California and attending Santa Monica College full-time in the evening. However, my life came to a complete halt due to an unexpected crisis, and I was forced to give up everything. On June 18th, 2001, the morning of my birthday, I received the devastating news of the sudden death of my grandmother Ida. This crisis deeply impacted my life and transformed me significantly through the shaping of my character. Additionally, it placed a profound new perspective on my entire life. I was at a standstill, her death caused me to reevaluate my life and paint a new picture on the canvas of life. She was my refuge, and when she died, she took a piece of my heart with her. Her death is a prime example of how fragile and precious life truly is. Life is a continual process of growth and change, and even though the process can be painful at times, it does bare rewards. After my rude awakening, I realized that I had a decision to make: I had to choose between everything I worked for in California and moving back to New York City to start all over.

I was at the crossroads in my life, and I needed healing to fill the huge void in my heart. I needed to be near my family in my time of mourning, and the only way to do that was to fly home to New York. Making the transition from one place in your life into the next can be very challenging; however the positive results that transpire from those challenges are priceless.

Emerge. Evolve. Transform. Transcend.

THE PRECIOUS GEM COLLECTION

I decided to move back to New York City on April 1st 2002, and what seemed like such a difficult task, quickly became simple as I began to lay the foundation for my future. Returning home was deeper than just communing with family and old friends, it was about overcoming a great challenge. I found comfort amongst family and friends, and that enabled me to find peace with the loss of my grandmother. During the time that I took off from school, I ventured into the working world to further pursue professional endeavors. In addition, not only did I grow professionally, but I was able to grow personally as well. I was able to gain the knowledge and tools necessary for me to succeed not only in the working world, but in the world at large. My professional experience afforded me the ability to cultivate my interests, exercise my skills, meet a wide array of people, and travel to places I have only dreamed of.

In this race we call life, we are often in a hurry to reach a certain destination, but we must realize that the race is not given to the swift, but to those who can endure it. I gave up everything that I had gained in Los Angeles, and I regained the strength to recapture my dream. After my grandmother died, I realized that I truly was not living my life to the fullest. I was like a bird caged and held back by fear. Her death was like a rebirth for me in a lot of ways, as I went from living a life filled with fear, to a life filled with adventure and discovery. I finally developed my wings, her death enabled me to fly and begin the next chapter of my life. Life grants an inexplicable amount of strength and courage. You never know just how far you can fly unless you try. If you can close your eyes, open your heart, and see life beyond the horizon, then you open yourself up to unlimited possibilities.

In life, we are faced with many challenges and these challenges are placed in our paths to build our strength and character. However, they tend to jade our focus, kill our dreams, dismiss our hope, and cloud our visions, but we must not succumb.

THE PRECIOUS GEM COLLECTION

LEAVE THE BAGGAGE BEHIND

We have all had regrets from relationships gone badly. However, it is up to us to leave the emotional baggage behind, and start fresh with a clean slate. We have all experienced love and pain. We have all been hurt, heartbroken, and disappointed in our dealings with people. However, we must not carry these emotions into new relationships. The first thing we tend to do is blame either ourselves, or the other party for the sour points in a failed relationship. However, all that does is leave the issues unresolved, and buried under more hurt and more pain. There is a root to every problem, and unless we uproot the negative and plant new and positive seeds, we will fall into our old ways. We hold on to negative habits, and repeat unhealthy patterns, which in essence leads us to make the same mistakes. We must first get right with ourselves by forgiving ourselves for our own shortcomings, accepting the results, and forgiving others. We must take the time to analyze from within, examine our own heart, and evaluate our very own behavior, chalking it up to being either healthy or dysfunctional. Gather up what you can from past relationships that will be of good assistance to you in the present and future, and leave the rest behind. Get rid of the unnecessary stuff and free yourself of excess baggage because it will only weigh you down.

We must spend time alone in order to get to know ourselves, this way we will be able to pin point our likes and dislikes. Time alone is very valuable and essential for living a healthier, happier life. Do not fear spending time alone Gems, because spending some time solitude will only benefit you. How can one fully participate or engage in a new, fulfilling, worthwhile and meaningful relationship if one does not know how to be happy alone? If you cannot be happy alone, you cannot expect to be happy with someone else. If we do not find fulfillment or happiness within ourselves, we only empower others to create, control and dictate our happiness and/or sorrow.

THE PRECIOUS GEM COLLECTION

That's too much power Gems! We all hold the power to be who we want to be, and the right to choose who we want to share our time, energy, space, and dreams with. Choose wisely.

THE PRECIOUS GEM COLLECTION

LOVE & HAPPINESS

This message is an intimate portrait of what love is on many levels. God is love. Love is patient. Love is kind. Love is selfless. Love is unconditional. Love covers a multitude of sins. Perfect love casts out fear. Love accepts. Love heals. Love changes. Love teaches. Love lends. Love leads. Love is powerful. Love is the greatest gift! One huge thing that love also does is forgive, and forgiveness may sometimes be the hardest thing to do. However, it is pertinent that we as human beings get to a place of love where we can forgive and let live, release and let go. Forgiveness means handing it over to a Higher Power, even though you may feel powerful enough to handle it yourself. Don't carry unnecessary burdens when God wants to cast all your cares upon Him. Free your mind, open your heart, and let peace rule in your hearts always.

Where does love dwell? Love dwells in a place within. Love lives in each of our hearts and souls. So often we look to external sources such as people, places and things to make us happy, and we fail to realize that it comes from within. Love is a huge part of our existence. It keeps us alive and thriving, without it we would perish. God is love. Everything that brings us joy in friendships, families, and careers are products of our very own contributions into these aspects of our lives. We are the love we desire, we are the love we deserve, and we are the love we receive. Love is a gift that just keeps on giving; it grows more and more when we give it away. It takes rain to make a flower grow, but it is God's love that keeps us alive and thriving. Live your life to the fullest gems, and let love reign!

THE PRECIOUS GEM COLLECTION

THE GREATEST MEDICINE, THE ULTIMATE CURE!

QUESTION: Do you know what the best remedy is for people who insist on blocking your shine and snuffing out your God given light?

ANSWER: It is the light of love!

Shine brighter, stay beautiful, love harder, and keep it moving!

It is said that the best revenge is success, let God handle all the rest. People who hate are miserable, lonely, insecure, and lost. They need love and light more than anything else. When people throw hate off on you, most often you will find that they really hate themselves. I have learned at an early age that the only person worth losing yourself over is, NO person walking this earth. You got to live and let live, give and give some more, forgive and be forgiven. It's a life-long process!

Don't worry about others and why they are so full of negativity, worry about yourself and pray for them. Be as fabulous as God made you to be, that'll really blow some wigs back. As long as God is in your heart, and all of your limbs are intact, don't waste your time slipping on or tripping off of someone else's negativity. We are all imperfect, and we live in an imperfect world. Do yourself a favor and let some light into your own world. In doing so, you give others permission to shine as you open the shades and pull the curtains back on love. Live and let live! Love is the light.

THE PRECIOUS GEM COLLECTION

EYES

The most amazing thing to me has always been seeing into the soul of another simply by looking into their eyes. So much can be said without even saying a word, sometimes words just get in the way.

Have you ever smiled with your eyes, or cried without shedding one tear? It's no joke what the essence of a human being can really bring to life. There are so many hurting people in the world, and while some walk around wearing their pain on their sleeves, others try to hide their pain. However, what I have come to realize is that the eyes never lie. So often we go about our daily routines, self-absorbed and focused on reaching our next destination, but do we really take the time to look into the soul of another? I am sure each and every single one of us is guilty of being too busy for even ourselves at times, but I wanted to let you all know that no matter what each of you may have to face daily, you are not alone. God is steady watching over His Word to perform it, and sending His angels to encamp around and about you each day. Don't give up the fight! Stand strong against every ill that seeks to beset you. Storms don't last always, and dark clouds will always pass away. Enjoy life! Enjoy each day!

You are beautiful, fearfully and wonderfully made!

THE PRECIOUS GEM COLLECTION

LIFE JOURNEY

Life is not a destination, it is a journey. On this journey of life, there will be many lessons for you to learn. Life is the greatest teacher! God is the only utensil you need and the best utensil you could ever have. In everything that you face in life, there is a lesson to be learned, and the experience itself is the greatest teacher. In every trial, there is a lesson. In every broken heart, there is a lesson. In every downfall, there is a lesson. In every death, there is a lesson. In every change, there is a lesson. In every farewell, there is a lesson. So whenever you are faced with tribulation, always remember that there is a blessing awaiting you in the form of a lesson.

"Trust in the Lord with all of your heart and lean not on your own understanding; In all your ways acknowledge Him, and He will make your paths straight. (Proverbs 3:5&6 NIV)

THE PRECIOUS GEM COLLECTION

LIVE IN THE MOMENT

So often we put money up for rainy days, save our best pair of shoes for that one special outing, wear our best outfit on that one special occasion, and anticipate tomorrow so much that we often forget about today. Live in the moment Gems, yesterday is gone, today is here, and tomorrow is what we hope for. Do not save your best for days to come, your best is designated for this very day, this very moment. Pamper yourselves, splurge on that outfit or new pair of shoes, go to that fancy restaurant, buy your dream home, purchase that new car, apply for that dream job, get that desired degree, marry the love of your life, travel the world, and most of all, follow your heart.

Be present in what is, confident in what's to come, and strive to meet your destiny with poise and grace.

Celebrate Today & Live It Up!

THE PRECIOUS GEM COLLECTION

NURTURE YOUR NATURE

It is the nature of the sun to rise, set, and shed light. It is the nature of an Oscine to sing. It is the nature of a flower to bloom. It is the nature of the rain to come down and water the earth. It is the nature of the billows to roll. It is the nature of the stars to shine at night. It is the nature of a lion to roar. It is the nature of the grass to grow. It is the nature of a mother to nurture a child. It is the nature of a tree to shed leaves in the fall. It is the nature of a butterfly to flutter. It is the nature of a performer to perform. It is the nature of a teacher to teach. It is the nature of a student to learn. It is the nature of a pilot to operate an aircraft in flight.

What is your nature? If it is in your nature to sing, write, teach, cook, host, speak, read, draw, dance, compose, direct, produce, act, encourage, love or heal, you must nurture your nature. Do what you love and set aside a special time to foster your aspirations. We all possess a gift of some sort, one that is ready to be stirred up. It is fashioned by God, and it lives on the inside of you! There is nothing too impossible to achieve, and there is no dream too big to fulfill. Whatever you hold in your heart that brings you extreme joy and that flows from your being naturally should be cultivated.

The very essence of who you are is a gift to the world. Dream, Reach, Seek, and Be Gems!

THE PRECIOUS GEM COLLECTION

ON TOP OF THE WORLD

There may be times in life when it seems as if the world is on your shoulders, and the weight of the world rests upon your soul. There may be times when it seems as if you are drowning in the ills of this world and can barely keep your head above it all. There may be times in life when you can't see clearly the path set before you and you feel like you have lost your way. There may be times in life when you have given all you had to make it through one more day and felt like you did not have enough to make it through tomorrow.

During these times Gems, you must stand, fight, and search deep within yourself to find that inner strength and hold on to it. You must find your peace and center it. You must find your courage and wear it like a cloak. You must find the love within and make it your anchor. You must hold on to your faith and believe even when common sense tells you not to. You must find your inner voice and listen carefully to what it says. You must trust yourself enough to know that you will make it through one more day. Most importantly, you must trust that God will carry you through every situation, guide you in the way that you should go, keep you as the apple of His eye, and hide you under the shadow of His wings. Only then will you see that you are really on top of the world!

THE PRECIOUS GEM COLLECTION

ONE DAY AT A TIME

Each day we awake and go about our daily routines, and we may not get an opportunity to stop and smell the roses. We pass by tons of people each day, and we may only get a smile from 1 out of every 10. However, that one smile may be all that we need to get through the day. So often we smile through a thousand tears and hold so much deep inside, but one would never know what is deep within another's soul unless they took the time to take a closer look. I do not know what each of you may have to face each day, or what your heart holds. However, I do know that you are precious jewels and should be treated as such. Take life one day at a time, and take each day one step at a time.

Keep smiling Gems, for you never know who is falling in love with your smile…

THE PRECIOUS GEM COLLECTION

PAMPER THYSELF!

Pampering should be an everyday occurrence, but we all know that it is hard to fit pampering into our schedules. Well Gems, now is the time to kick back and relax. Take a few minutes to think about a couple of things that bring you joy and satisfaction. Whether it is taking a walk, grocery shopping, splurging on a pair of shoes, watching a basketball game, listening to music, walking the dog, reading a book, meditating, cooking dinner, or simply napping, we have to find a way to fit life's simple pleasures into our busy schedules each day. It may seem like an impossible venture, but it is well worth it. Pamper yourself Precious Gems, it's a must!

THE PRECIOUS GEM COLLECTION

POWER & STRENGTH IN EVERY STRUGGLE

In this life we will be faced with trials, and there may be times when we are standing face to face with adversity. However, I want you to know that there is power and strength in every struggle. The power and the presence of God will always reign supreme in our lives, because He is a very present help in times of trouble. There may be times when you feel like you are holding on by a mere thread and when your breakthrough seems distant. However, that is when you need to hold on tighter. You must take hold of your strength and know that even when you are weak, God's power is made strong. You must tighten your grip on peace and snatch joy up by the collar.

It may seem like you are walking this road alone at times, but God is with you always, as He promised to never leave you or forsake you. People may fail you or turn their backs on you, but God is always available to you. He is omnipresent, omniscient, and omnipotent. We live in a world that grows colder and colder each day, and it may seem like you can't win. However, if you believe, you can do *all* things through Christ which strengthens you. You have the most powerful weapon in your possession; you have a love that can combat any fiery dart, overcome any challenge, jump over any hurdle, and step over any stumbling block. We serve a mighty God who is able to do immeasurably more than we could ever ask or imagine according to His power that is at work within us.

"No weapon formed against you shall prosper." (Isaiah 54:7-NIV)
"So do not fear, for I am with you; do not be dismayed, for I am your God. I will strengthen you and help you; I will uphold you with my righteous right hand." (Isaiah 41:10 -NIV)

Emerge. Evolve. Transform. Transcend.

THE PRECIOUS GEM COLLECTION

PROMISES

How many times have promises been made and broken, leaving you hurt, disappointed, and confused? Well, I am here to tell you that there is one promise that shall never be broken, and that is God's promise to never leave you or forsake you. He will guide, instruct, and teach you in the way that you should go. He will keep you as the apple of His eye, and hide you under the shadow of His mighty wings. He will fight for you if you remain still (Exodus 14:14-NIV), for He is a very present help in times of trouble. "Those who hope in the Lord will renew their strength. They will soar on wings like eagles; they will run and not grow weary, they will walk and not be faint." (Isaiah 40:31-NIV) All of these promises are sealed by God and shall never be broken.

I am sure that we have all had promises broken, but it is even better to know that we serve a mighty God who stands by His every word. "As for God, his way is perfect; the word of the Lord is flawless. He is a shield for all who take refuge in Him." (2 Samuel 22:31-NIV) "God is not a man that He should lie, nor a son of man that He should change His mind. Does He speak and then not act? Does He promise and not fulfill?" (Numbers 23:19-NIV) We are human and capable of human error, but God is infallible and made perfect in every way. We are fearfully and wonderfully made in Christ and no matter how many times we fall or how many mistakes we make, God still loves us and keeps us in the palm of His mighty hand. There is nothing that can separate us from the love of God. So stand firm on His promises Gems, and trust Him to do all that He said he would do. God's got it!

"Your word is a lamp unto my feet and a light for my path." (Psalms 119:105-NIV)

THE PRECIOUS GEM COLLECTION

RESTORATION

Many have suffered from either the effects of a broken spirit, a broken heart, a broken home, or a broken vision. Dreams may have been shattered, promises may have been broken, and hope may have been lost along the way. There may have been times when you felt like it was too hard to endure a test or trial because the pain was unbearable. However, that is when God is carrying you. Things fall apart sometimes, just so that they can be put back together even stronger and ten times better. It may not be in your power to fix it. It may be out of your hands to serve a greater purpose, and that is when God is working it out and working His Master Plan. "And we know that in all things God works for the good of those who love God, to those who have been called according to His purpose. (Romans 8:28-NIV) "Therefore, there is now no condemnation for those who are in Christ Jesus."(Romans 8:1-NIV)

There is nothing too great for God to handle, for He is greater than any problem or any situation you may have to face. He is able to do immeasurably more than you could ever ask or imagine according to His power that is at work within you. He is the creator, and He knows all things. He is omnipotent, omniscient, and omnipresent.

"For those God foreknew he also predestined to be conformed to the likeness of His Son, that he might be the firstborn among many brothers. And those he predestined, he also called; those he called, he also justified; those he justified, he also glorified." (Romans 8:29, 30-NIV) So if God created you, then He knows what is best for you, even when it does not appear that way. Even when things are broken down, torn apart, and shattered beyond belief, God is working on your behalf. Don't look at the situation with your physical eye; look at it through the eyes of faith. God is in control and He holds all power in His hand, and He will uphold you with His righteous hand.

THE PRECIOUS GEM COLLECTION

"And I will restore to you the years that the locust hath eaten, the cankerworm, and the caterpillar, and the palmerworm, my great army which I sent among you. You will have plenty to eat, until you are full, and you will praise the name of the Lord your God, who has worked wonders for you; never again will my people be shamed." (Joel 2:25&26-NIV)

God can and He will fix it!

THE PRECIOUS GEM COLLECTION

RIDE THE WAVE

Sometimes life has a funny way of sweeping us off of our feet and carrying us to places that we would have never imagined. Life's unexpected twists and turns find a way to take us down paths that we may have never took the initiative to tread upon. However, after we arrive at a certain place, we find ourselves in a state of inexplicable joy. What I have learned in my years spent on this earth is that when something viewed as negative occurs in my life, the end result is always positive. When tragedy strikes, or even when things do not go the way I planned, I have learned to be still and ride the wave because there is a bigger plan at hand. It is not always easy to go with the flow, but I have found that it does allow one to embrace the peace that is held within. We live in a frigid world, and sometimes life can hit us with a low blow that may seem impossible to block. However, if one continues to stand with feet firmly planted, one will never reap defeat.

Ride the wave Gems, you will reach the shore in peace. You are more than conquerors!

CHAPTER 2

***

EVOLVE

THE PRECIOUS GEM COLLECTION

SEASONS CHANGE

As I walk around outside and the cool breeze brushes against my face, I cannot help but to smell a change in the air. As I step on the leaves that have fallen from the trees, I am reminded that a new season is soon approaching. As I look at my surroundings, I cannot help but to notice all of the different people wearing heavy coats, decorative scarves, designer hats, and galoshes. The rain stains the ground as it falls down upon us, and the water nourishes the grass enabling it to sprout. The flower beds are kissed with sunlight after the heavy rains, and the birds find their nesting place in a place high above ground. The squirrels scurry about in search for their daily bread, and the twigs lay on the ground awaiting a lighter step. People walk around outside looking up at the morning sky, and they breathe a sigh of relief because it is the dawn of a new day.

It is not always easy making the transition from one phase of your life into the next. However, change is constant, and we must all turn the page to a new chapter at one point or another. Change may be uncomfortable at times, and it may not always be expected. However, it is something that we must welcome in order to evolve into the individuals that we are destined to be. We have recently entered into a New Year and embarked on a new journey. What every New Year signifies to me is a "New Beginning". Each New Year gives us an opportunity to reflect on the past year and set new goals in motion. Each season gives us an opportunity to sow new seeds and reap the good harvest. It is also a time for us to celebrate life and look forward to another year ahead of us. While one may never know what to expect throughout the course of a year, you can always hope for the best. Stay focused and have faith that everything will fall into place the way that it's supposed to.

May you always remember that the sky is the limit and that life provides us with endless possibilities Gems. The power of God within us is unlimited!

THE PRECIOUS GEM COLLECTION

SPEAK LIFE TO IT!
"Do you not yet understand that whatever enters the mouth goes into the stomach and is eliminated? But those things which proceed out of the mouth come from the heart and they defile a man." (Matthew 15:17&18-NIV)

The power of life and death lives in the tongue, and with words, we have the power to create things. There may be things in your life that may appear to be dead in your eyes, but we have the ability in Christ to awaken those things that are dormant by speaking life to them. Sometimes we lack the faith that would enable us to accomplish what we set out to achieve. In turn, we lose hope in those things which are deemed impossible, and we are hindered by the stumbling block of doubt in our way. *So Jesus said to them, "Because of your unbelief; for assuredly, I say to you, if you have faith as little as a mustard seed, you will say to this mountain, 'Move from here to there', and it will move; and nothing will be impossible for you." (Matthew 17:20-NIV)*

God has placed something on the inside of each and every one of us, and it will require faith to cultivate and produce what He has deposited. Don't give up or throw in the towel when it does not look like a prayer has been answered, or that progress has been made in the area of your life where you desire it most. God is an on time God, and His timing is impeccable. Sometimes a delay is a blessing in disguise. There may be things in your life that have been dead for far too long, and it's time that they are awakened by the Holy Spirit.

SPEAK LIFE into that relationship! *SPEAK LIFE* into that child! *SPEAK LIFE* into those finances! *SPEAK LIFE* into that friendship! *SPEAK LIFE* into those limbs! *SPEAK LIFE* into your soul! *SPEAK LIFE* into your career! *SPEAK LIFE* into your family! *SPEAK LIFE* into your home! *SPEAK LIFE* into your spirit!

SPEAK LIFE TO IT GEMS, AWAKEN THAT LIFE ENERGY!

THE PRECIOUS GEM COLLECTION

STRIDES IN THE RIGHT DIRECTION

Breath of life is a wonderful gift to behold. Even though we may not be able to clearly see the path that is set before us, we must trust that with each step guidance will follow. One may never know what the day will bring forth or what tomorrow may hold, all you have to do is take strides in the right direction.

There may be times when it seems like you are walking blindly through this life and that the road is not clearly marked for the journey ahead of you. However, you must remember that God will be your eyes when you cannot see, your ears when you cannot hear, your feet when you cannot walk, your road map when you have lost your way, your shield in the midst of every battle, a lamp unto your feet, a light unto your path, your strength when you are weak, your peace in the midst of chaos, your hope when you feel all hope is lost, your courage when you are afraid, your wisdom when you lack understanding, your joy when you are in pain, and most of all, the love that will sustain you throughout eternity.

"The LORD is my shepherd; I shall not want. He maketh me to lie down in green pastures: he leadeth me beside the still waters. He restoreth my soul: he leadeth me in the paths of righteousness for his name's sake. Yea, though I walk through the valley of the shadow of death, I will fear no evil: for thou art with me; thy rod and thy staff they comfort me. Thou preparest a table before me in the presence of mine enemies: thou anointest my head with oil; my cup runneth over. Surely goodness and mercy shall follow me all the days of my life: and I will dwell in the house of the LORD forever." (Psalms 23-KJV)

THE PRECIOUS GEM COLLECTION

SUNSHINE AFTER THE RAIN

There may be times when you are in the midst of a storm and it seems like there is no shield from the rain. There may be times when you feel like the rain is just pouring down over your life and that you are susceptible to drowning. There may be times when it seems as if the rain just won't cease and that the storm is boundless and endless. There may be times when the tears flow endlessly from your eyes and your vision may be blurred. Well I am here to tell you that there is sunshine after the rain and a rainbow after every storm. Wipe away those tears and rejoice, for sunshine is on the way. If you are facing a difficult time and you feel like all hope is lost, trust your faith and be strong, God will carry you along. Character and strength are being built, and you are being made whole.

THE PRECIOUS GEM COLLECTION

BEAUTIFUL ESSENCE

What would life be like if the sun didn't shine, the birds didn't sing, the stars fell out of the sky, the seasons didn't change, and dreams never came alive? The little things in life that matter the most are usually the things that are overlooked and taken for granted. We live in a world where technology far exceeds nature. We are now way more dependent on gadgets, rather than those things which are innately connected to the essence of who we are. We focus so much on society's standard of living that we forget who we are in a sense. What would the world be like without cars, computers, and cable? Would we still be able to maintain the standard of living that we currently uphold? Some might say that the world as a whole would not be able to function, and would be in total state of disarray. We only hold on to this notion because we have become accustomed to the "new & improved" way of doing things. It wasn't long ago when word-of-mouth was the mode of communication used for correspondence. There was also a time when there were no color televisions, and films were in black in white. There was a natural tendency to travel on foot, and you were not looked down upon for not having the latest motor-driven vehicle. Cellular phones were a luxury, not a necessity. You weren't identified by the clothes you wore, or the position you held. Nowadays, people rarely respect you for who you are, but rather for how you appear. The world we live in has changed greatly over time, and as time goes by, even greater changes will occur. It is up to us to find middle ground so that we do not go too far to the left, or to the right. It is not always easy to make a smooth transition into a new era, but change is inevitable. There is always room for improvement and adjustment once the change occurs. Don't get caught up in the hype because all that glitters is not gold. What happens when what you aspire to is no longer a reflection of who you are or what God intended for you to be? We often feel that if we don't alter our appearances and personalities to match society's blueprint, we are doomed. It is okay to want to better yourself or make improvements on your persona. However, when it totally

Emerge. Evolve. Transform. Transcend.

THE PRECIOUS GEM COLLECTION

omits the core of your being, you can end up doing major damage, and also run the risk of losing yourself in the midst. However, once you realize that who you are will create a space for you in this world, you won't expend so much energy trying to fit into a mold that you have either outgrown, or simply do not belong to. You won't sway back and forth like waves trying to fit in. There is no one who can fill your shoes. Even if an exact replica was made of you, it would not come close to your unique and carefully crafted essence. You are created in the image and likeness of God. Embrace yourself, love yourself, and relish in your uniqueness. There is only one you, and who you are is beautiful!

THE PRECIOUS GEM COLLECTION

COMMIT THY WORK

Stop competing, stay in your lane, and run your own race. So often we get discouraged because we are busy paying attention to what others are doing, where others are, and where they are going. All the while, we should be focused on ourselves. We need to spend more time focused on how we can get by in this life by doing the things that God predestined us to do. Of course we are going to look at the lives of others and admire them. However, we must realize that God made each of us in His image and likeness. He gave each of us a unique set of tools to work with. Imagine if we were all made to look, act, walk, and talk the same. What kind of world would this be? A very dull and boring world I presume. There would be no need for different professions, because we would all be doing the same thing. There would be no need for different languages, because we would all speak the same language. There would be no need for different colors; there would be one basic color for everything. What about diversity? There would be none! We would be walking around looking like robots. "Before I formed thee in the belly I knew thee; and before thou camest forth out of the womb I sanctified thee, and I ordained thee a prophet unto the nations."(Jeremiah 1:5-KJV) God knew exactly what He was doing when He set us apart before we were even formed in the womb. "For I know the thoughts that I think toward you, saith the LORD, thoughts of peace, and not of evil, to give you an expected end. Then shall ye call upon me, and ye shall go and pray unto me, and I will hearken unto you. And ye shall seek me, and find me, when ye shall search for me with all your heart."(Jeremiah 29:11-13-KJV) He set aside a special purpose for each of us. Trust that God has a Master Plan, for He is the Master Planner. He is working it out for you! The Master is always at work, and He is able to do immeasurably more than we could ever ask or imagine according to His power that is at work within us. "Commit thy works unto the LORD, and thy thoughts shall be established."(Proverbs 16:3-KJV)

THE PRECIOUS GEM COLLECTION

FEAR

Growing up my parents would always say, "Have your own mind and be a leader." It became a huge part of my existence, as I began to walk, talk, think and exist like a leader, not only because my parents said so, but because of what God placed on the inside of me. Trust me when I tell you that it is not always easy to walk in front and be a leader, because it requires an immense amount of poise, grace and humility. If we look at some of the great leaders of our time, you will see that their woeful plight was not sought after by many because of the huge responsibility associated with the role. However, it takes a good leader to lead a lost people, or people who are simply looking to model themselves after someone positive who can lead them in the right direction, rather than lead them astray. Christ paid a high price because He shed His own blood so that we may receive salvation and have eternal life. Who on earth do you know that will hang, bleed, and die on the cross for your sins? He did it once and for ALL! We are free to live and be who God created us to be. We are free to let our lights so shine because Christ paid it all at Calvary. WE ARE FREE!

The only thing that binds us is fear, and why should we fear when Christ has given us the spirit of love, power, and a sound mind? We have authority over darkness, and over all the power of the enemy. Fear does not always have to be brought about by something tangible, it can be the fear in our minds, an illusion that keeps us from forward progression. The fear in our mind holds us back from achieving our goals. Fear keeps us incarcerated, and it tries so hard to take away our God given right to be free.

Have you ever stopped yourself from applying from a job because they required certain qualifications, and you felt as if you did not meet their standards? Have you ever turned down an invitation to a prestigious event because you felt like you were not "prestigious" enough? Have you ever been called on in class to give an answer, but you failed to answer because you were unsure of yourself, only to have someone else give the same answer you had in mind and it was correct? Have you ever dreamed of doing

THE PRECIOUS GEM COLLECTION

something all of your life, but because one person told you that you were not capable, or that your dream was impossible to achieve, you gave up on your dream? Have you ever wanted to say something to someone, but because you were afraid of what their response might be, you retreated and went back into your shell, only to find out later that they would have received you with open arms and an open heart? You get my drift Gems, we have all backed down, backed up, and backed away from many things because of fear. However, we must realize that fear is an illusion. It exists first in your mind, and then it manifests into your actions. It becomes full grown and spreads out all over your life if you allow it to. Fear is deadly, and instead of letting it kill us, we must kill it! It is amazing how much more we could do as human beings if we banished fear from our minds. Fear cripples us and it leaves us bound by images that we have created in our mind. It handicaps us in a way that debilitates us. God is the only one who can help us overcome our fears, but we must take the first step of faith by letting go and letting God. You know that God will never leave you or forsake you, as He promised from the very beginning. There is nothing to it but to do it!

Fret not upon things you have no control over, instead do your best to change the things you can control. God will do the rest!

THE PRECIOUS GEM COLLECTION

GOD HAS NOT FORGOTTEN

No matter how bleak your situation may appear, always remember that God is working behind the scenes to bring together the people, places, and things that will play a part in your deliverance from a desert experience. It may look like things are not working out, but God says that all things work together for the good of those who love Him, and who are called according to His purpose. God is not a man that He should lie, nor the son of man that He should change His mind. I am a living witness of God's ability to perform all that He has promised. He is a Master Planner, and He is working His Master Plan in each and every one of our lives. He is the potter and we are the clay.

Do not focus on your situation with your physical eye, place your attention on what can be seen through your spiritual eye. We are to walk by faith and not by sight, for it is through the eyes of faith that we will be able to see God's Mighty hand at work in everything. Do not get me wrong, I know that it may not always be easy to trust in the Lord with all of your heart and lean not on your own understanding when chaos and mayhem surrounds you. However, we know that the VICTORY is ours. We are more than conquerors in Christ, and He will see to it that we succeed. He has equipped us with every tool necessary to win the good fight of faith, and He is with us every step of the way. For we know that the battle is not ours, it is the Lord's! This should give us the confidence to stand against every fiery dart, even when all else falters. It may not always be easy to stand Gems, but it will most definitely make us stronger, and build character. The one thing that is certain is the fact that God loves us unconditionally, and He promised to never leave us or forsake us. People may turn their backs on you, but that is not your concern because God says that vengeance is His, and He shall repay. Do not worry about all those who say "nay," for as long as God is in your corner, you are in business. Take heed to what you hear. You do not need to take counsel from fools, nor do you need to sit amongst those who take pleasure in folly. The road is not easy, nor is the path always a smooth one.

THE PRECIOUS GEM COLLECTION

However, you can rest assured that God's grace alone is sufficient. He is able to do immeasurably above and beyond what we could ever ask or imagine according to His power that is at work within us. His mercy endures forever. God is unchanging. He is the same yesterday, today, and forever. He is the Alpha and the Omega. He is the great I AM. Trust Him!

THE PRECIOUS GEM COLLECTION

THE POWER OF PRAYER

After you have exhausted all of your possibilities by seeking the counsel of friends, and done all the crying you could possibly do, you still have another option. The option left open to you at all times is prayer. The power of prayer goes far beyond what you can imagine because it allows you to call on the Creator and call forth the power that is already deposited on the inside of you. Greater is He who is in you for a reason, and one reason is so that you never run out of options.

God should be our first option, but I know that there are times when the support of a physical being really brings comfort. I have called on family and friends for answers many times, but the reality is that they are not God. I thank God for those friends and family members who are there to be my shoulder when I am weak and an open ear when I just need someone to listen. We all need someone in our corner, and it truly is a blessing to have them near. However, we must be careful not put our friends and family in God's rightful place. He is the author and finisher of our faith, and just as He gives our friends and family over to us, He can very well separate us from them in order to accomplish in us what He set out to accomplish. God is a jealous God, and He wants us to keep Him first. For this reason, I have learned to take inventory and really examine where God really sits in my life. Is He on my left when He should be on my right? Does He get pushed off onto the back burner often? Is He in the front row seat of my life? We must be careful not to make people our gods. God is the only one who deserves all the glory and honor. It is always comforting to be able to pick up a phone and call on those you love for support and encouragement. However, what about when no one is home? What about when you need an answer right away and there is no one around? What about when you get a busy signal? Are you going to give up, or are you going to call on your Father in Heaven who is *always* available to you? God's line is never busy, and He will never turn you away. His hotline is open 24/7, and it's free Gems!

Emerge. Evolve. Transform. Transcend.

THE PRECIOUS GEM COLLECTION

Now don't get it twisted Gems, you may not always get the answer that you want or that you thought you were going to get, but it will always be the *best* answer. God will never lead you astray, nor will He give you a false response. He is infallible, perfect in every single way.

Of course there are times when we doubt and become consumed by fear. However, when you know, that you know, that you know that God is your protector, your provider, your healer, your redeemer, your refuge, and your fortress, you will never hesitate to make the call. Don't cling to people when you can cling to Him. Don't leech onto people when you can leech onto Him. Don't lose your head over people, but instead give your heart to Him. He is a very present help in times of trouble. Call on Him Gems! He is awaiting your call, and His lines are open just for you. He is an awesome God!

THE PRECIOUS GEM COLLECTION

LOVE IT, LEAVE IT, and LET IT GO...

Have you ever loved someone so much that you could not bear the thought of their absence? However, did you suddenly get a wake-up call and realize that the one you may be holding on so tightly to is not right for you, or perhaps not ready for you? Have you ever found yourself at a crossroads trying to figure out where you belong or where you went wrong?

So Gems, what do you do when faced with a situation where you love someone, but you know it is best to leave them alone, and let it go? You must stand firm on your faith, love and respect yourself, and keep strutting along. You are a precious jewel, and you are worth far more than rubies. Always remember that everyone who enters your life, enters it is for a reason, season, or lifetime. There is a lesson for you to learn, and they are the teachers. It may even be the reverse, and you may even be there to teach them a valuable lesson. It has been said that "when the student is ready, the teacher will appear." This statement is very profound because it reminds us that sometimes we think we know what we may want, or that we are ready for certain aspects of our lives to unfold. However, we may not be ready, or the timing is just not right. It is sometimes hard to remember that God is in control, even when you feel you have such a handle on life. This goes for anything we face in life, be it love, loss, or gain. If you hold onto anything too tight, you run the risk of smothering it. If you loosen your grip and set it free, you return it to its natural state. A state of peace and clarity evokes a certain harmony, causing all things to work together for good. In essence, what you may want may not be what you need, but what you need may turn out to be what you want.

THE PRECIOUS GEM COLLECTION

MAKE ROOM FOR LOVE & LET LOVE REIGN!

Have you ever walked around all day like your program was held together, but all the while you were crying on the inside and hoping that just somebody, anybody would see your anguish and pain? Have you ever walked around all day wearing an "S" on your chest doing the most, but all the while you want to take the "S" and shove it? Do you ever rush home after completing your daily activities and realize that you are rushing home to dead silence, an answering machine with blinking zeroes letting you know that no one even cares enough to call simply to say hello. However, when you do get a message, is it from people who just want to dump their crap and drama on you for you to dispose of it on top of your own crap and drama? Or, do you rush home to sit alone in your humble abode anticipating tomorrow, while trying to erase yesterday's pain? Well, I am here to tell you that if you fit the description, I have a remedy for you!

You have a choice, so what are you going to choose? What should you choose? You can sit and wallow in self-pity, or you can sing a new tune. Precious Gems, what will it be? Choose to sing about love and all that it can be as well as add to your life. Choose to fantasize about the days when your answering machine will be filled with pleasant tones and sincere wishes. Choose to forgive yourself for allowing your life to be a waste basket for everyone else's trash, and for serving as a doormat that says "WELCOME" to intruders who in essence are not welcome. Choose to forget the past, and go full force into your future. Choose to breathe, relax, and dream of a better day and a better life, a life even better than the life you live now. Choose to live in the moment, and allow yesterday to slowly fade away. Choose to focus on today and see your life clearly as your grandest blessing. Release yourself from pain and open the way for love, peace, and joy to reign. Let go of fear, and allow clarity, strength, courage, and wisdom to remain.

THE PRECIOUS GEM COLLECTION

NEW BEGINNINGS

I am sure we have all heard someone utter that nothing in life is guaranteed. Well Gems, I beg to differ, because we know that God is the same yesterday, today, and forever. That's one true guarantee that we can hold firm to. We can rest assured that as the seasons change, the Lord remains the same. Another guarantee in life is the fact that things will change, they don't stay the same. What a blessing it is to know that the Word of the Lord is living and active, it shall never pass away. The earth may fall away, but God's Word is constant. His Word is magnified above His name and His Word is settled in Heaven. So with all of this in mind, we can celebrate change and *New Beginnings* with hearts full of joy, because we know that God provided us new opportunities for enjoyment. It is so easy to get caught up with the way things used to be, how we thought they would be, and how we think they should be. We must cast off our old way of thinking in order for God to do a *new* thing. We will go through many changes in life, but these changes are set in motion in order to get us to come out of our comfort zones and into the place God predestined for us. It is not always easy to embrace change, but we must accept it in order for God to fulfill His purpose in our lives. He promised to never leave you or forsake you, so when you are treading upon unfamiliar territory, trust that God is with you. He has sent an angel before you to prepare the way, and He will hide you under the shadow of His wings. Move forward in faith. Trust that the Lord has prepared something new and wonderful for you. He wants you to grow in Him. He wants to take you to new levels, but He requires your trust. You must have a willing heart and a willing spirit. He has not given you the spirit of fear, but of love, power, and a sound mind. Take heed and be receptive to Him. Open your heart to receive His messages, for He will never lead you astray. God loves His children and wants the absolute best for us. As He wraps His loving arms around you and fills your heart with an abundance of His love, embrace Him Gems.

THE PRECIOUS GEM COLLECTION

Take hold of His hand and walk with Him. Let Him whisper in your ear as you listen closely to what He is saying. He will put a new song in your mouth. Sing it with all of your might. Cry out to Him in your time of need. Call on Him and He will answer. Give Him your burdens and cast all of your cares on Him, for His yoke is easy and His burden is light. You don't have to carry them. They are not meant for you to carry. Hand them over to the Lord and let Him take care of you. Accept the things you cannot change and change the things you can. Forgive and let go of unnecessary weights. They will only bring you down and take away your strength. Hold firmly to your joy, for the joy of the Lord is your strength. Let Him fight the battle for you. The battle is not yours, it's the Lord's. Be still and know that He is God. Have faith and trust in the Lord. May God be with you always.

THE PRECIOUS GEM COLLECTION

PUT ON THE RIGHT HAT!

In life, we may have to wear more than one hat. The hat of humility, grace, peace, joy, patience, meekness, endurance, perseverance, kindness, victory, courage, armor, wisdom, faith, discernment, and of course the hat that always wins, the hat of love.

The reason for this Gems, is because we will encounter many different things in life that will require a different response. There is a time to act, and a time to be still. We most often will need the hat of grace to keep us from reacting or overreacting. We need the hat of humility so that we don't become arrogant or self-righteous. We need the hat of peace so that we can maintain composure even in situations where chaos and mayhem may surround us. We need the hat of joy, because the joy of the Lord is our strength. We need the hat of patience so that we will able to wait on the Lord and not faint or become weary in doing good. We need the hat of meekness so that we may be sensitive to the needs of others. We need the hat of endurance to sustain us in the midst of every storm and through every trial that we may face. We need the hat of perseverance to overcome any challenges we may face. We need the hat of kindness to ensure that our spirits stay sweet and our lights shine. We need the hat of courage, to fight the good fight of faith. We need the hat of discernment to see clearly what God is showing or speaking to us. We need the full armor of God because we war not against flesh and blood, but against principalities of darkness. We need the hat of wisdom so that we may be able to discern and gain insight into the things of God. We need the hat of faith because the just shall live by faith. We need the hat of victory because in Christ we are more than conquerors and the victory is already ours. Most of all, we need the hat of love to keep us firmly planted and rooted in the things of God, for above all, God is the ultimate reflection of love.

THE PRECIOUS GEM COLLECTION

RESTORE YOUR SOUL

I want to reiterate three important things to you in this inspiration. The three R's involved in survival and maintenance. RESTORATION, REJUVENATION and RENEWAL are three major keys to staying fit in life. To be whole in mind, body and soul is very important to achieving any type of success. We get so caught up moving and shaking, so much so that we often forget to rest. It is pertinent that every human being gains the rest that is essential for longevity in this race called life, or else one will have to sit on the sidelines while everyone else is running the race.

We all want to get to the finish line, but we have to be prepared. I want to encourage you all to take the time to rest, relax and regroup. You don't want to run around on empty and then crash, nor do you want to be stuck on the side of the road waiting for a boost when you could have taken preventative measures. Do the things you like to do and don't normally get a chance to do. Whether it is on the weekend or a day off from work, take the time to do YOU! Routine can become very tiresome and monotonous, and we all need a little break every now and then. It does wonders for your soul, and it also equips you with even more energy to tackle each new day. Go to the beach. Listen to the ocean roar. Watch the billows roll. Take in the sights. Stop and smell the roses. Walk in the sand. Watch the sunrise and sunset. Feed the birds. Get reacquainted with your inner-self, and listen to what your spirit may be whispering to you. Do all the things that bring you joy and inner peace.

THE PRECIOUS GEM COLLECTION

THE CHOICE IS YOURS

I realized something very profound after conversing with my dad, and it really blows my mind every time I am presented with this truth. We have a choice in everything that we do, a God given choice. We are going to be faced with challenges, but it is how we respond to those challenges that will determine the outcome and our progression. It is not always easy to choose life, happiness, love and victory over death, sorrow, hate and defeat. However, we still have a choice and the choice is ours to make.

Choose life this day! Choose love this day! Choose freedom this day! Choose beauty this day! Choose joy this day! Choose peace this day! Choose growth this day! Choose happiness this day! Choose forgiveness this day! Choose truth this day! Choose victory this day! CHOOSE LIFE!   We are more than conquerors!

The road is not always easy, nor is it always laced with ribbons and roses, but it is paved with an abundance of God's love and that is enough to sustain us!

THE PRECIOUS GEM COLLECTION

THE STORMS OF LIFE

I know that at times it may feel like no one understands or could possibly understand what you go through on the inside, but trust me when I tell you that God knows. You have been striving so hard and for so very long, and sometimes it may seem as if your plight is never ending. You sit still waiting for the rainbow to appear after every storm, only to find more dark clouds forming over your life. It seems as if everyone around you is succeeding in their most sought after endeavors, and there you sit awaiting your chance of liberation; waiting for your chance to be and walk in the fullness of who God created you to be. Believe me when I tell you I know how it feels to be surrounded by family and friends who don't even look close enough to see that your heart is breaking. I know how it feels to be a rose amidst thorns. I know how it feels to dream, hope, seek, and wish to find the answer that seems so far out of reach, and sometimes nowhere to be found. Believe me when I tell you that I know how it feels to hold so much love inside that it overwhelms you, but you can't even give it away because the world is so cold. I know how it feels to pray and cry out hoping that just one day God will hear and answer immediately. I know how it feels to have a broken spirit and broken heart, and then realize that you are the only one who can do the work in order for healing to prevail. Trust me when I tell you I know! Life is not easy, but the storms of life shield us in some mysterious and beautiful way. Storms teach us how to stand on our own two feet. Storms teach us how to run when we want to faint. Storms prepare us for the good that God has in store for us. Storms serve as breeding ground for VICTORY! Storms teach us how to fight the good fight of faith and win. Storms take the dark clouds that form over our lives and make room for sunshine to come our way. Storms bring forth growth, transformation, cleansing and healing. Where would we be without the storms of life? We would not be ready for the awesome life that God has in store for us, and believe me Gems, He wants us to be ready. He loves us that much!

THE PRECIOUS GEM COLLECTION

TRANSFORMATION

One thing that is certain in life, is the fact that change is inevitable, inescapable, and ineluctable. As the seasons change, we as human beings change. For this very reason, we must accept the things that we cannot change, and do our very best to change the things that we can. God created the seasons, and there is a season for every activity under the sun. In addition, while change is a constant force in life, it can sometimes be uncomfortable. While the many things in life that are good for us may bring forth a bit of discomfort, we must rest assured that the process will bring forth God's desired end result.

There may be times when you feel as if the world is crashing down on you, or that you cannot bear to endure yet another change. However, you must realize that you are equipped to endure as long as you are granted breath of life. No one ever said that the road would be easy, but it definitely is an essential part of life to endure these sorts of changes, be it good or bad. You may have to deal with internal conflict because it is a natural tendency to want to fight against change or the discomfort associated with it. It is normal for one to want to stay in a comfort zone and hold on to the "security blanket" that has provided much comfort and satisfaction along the way. However, that same comfort zone can counteract your growth process, and leave you stagnate. Change not only brings about growth, but it also allows your character to be developed. The strength that you gain during this process will enable you to weather the storms of life. One must be prepared for each phase of their life. While we may want things to stay the same, we must realize that we as humans are bound to evolve and transform throughout our entire lives, therefore causing our situations and circumstances to change. The change first occurs within, and the changes that occur on the inside may sometimes disrupt everything around you, and vice versa. Change shakes up the things you are very much accustomed to, and it often causes another part of you to emerge.

Emerge. Evolve. Transform. Transcend.

THE PRECIOUS GEM COLLECTION

As things change, you are enabled to grow and enter into another realm of maturity. Anything that enables you to proceed into the next phase of your life is always a good thing. There is not one thing that you face in life that you are not prepared for. From the moment we are conceived and brought into this world, we undergo a series of changes. From embryo to adult, your life will most certainly change. However, each phase prepares you for the chapters of your life that follow. Change is a wonderful thing and should be welcomed with an open heart and open mind. Don't run from change; instead embrace it with all that you are. Enjoy the seasons of your life, knowing that with each new season, a new and wonderful part of you will be unveiled.

THE PRECIOUS GEM COLLECTION

WONDERFULLY MADE

As human beings, we have a tendency to downplay our strengths and validate our weaknesses. It is so much easier for us to believe the negative than it is for us to believe the positive aspects of who we are. Is it possible to give ourselves compliments without being egotistical or arrogant? Of course! We are fearfully and wonderfully made in the image and likeness of Christ. What does this mean? This means that we have been granted the right to feel good, look good, be good, and live good. It's all good with God! As long as you maintain a humble heart, it is okay to give yourself a pat on the back. Give all Glory to God and allow Him to continue molding and shaping wonderful you. He is not done yet Gems, the best is yet to come!

The outer shell is a mere covering to the beautiful essence that lives within. It is not what's on the outside that makes the lasting impression; it's what lies at the core that lasts. Your heart and soul are treasures and the deepest part of whom and what *you* are lives there. Look deep inside yourself and embrace every, single, precious part of you.

It is often said that a first impression is a lasting impression, but the last impression is the one we are left with, so do your best to make it count!

THE PRECIOUS GEM COLLECTION

FOOD FOR THOUGHT***RENEW YOUR MIMD

It is very, very, very important that what we consume is suitable for us. We can easily get caught up in making what we are accustomed to our first choice because it is convenient. However, we must realize that sometimes what's convenient and easy is not always the better choice. It becomes so much harder to train ourselves to go for what is better for us, rather than for what is easy, accessible and convenient. We do damage to ourselves by not taking inventory of what we consume. It's time to take inventory!

As humans, it is so much easier for us to soak up the negative words we hear, and meditate on negative thoughts because we operate so much like sponges. It is rare that one will give more attention to the positive, unless their mind is trained to do so. We are always so hard on ourselves because we live in a hard society that puts so much emphasis on the superficial. This in turn makes us self-conscious. We then start to focus more on what is going on outside of ourselves, rather than on what's happening within. We start to do any and everything to make ourselves into what society has deemed to be "authentic" and "acceptable". We forget who we are and where we come from. We get all frazzled if we do not look like society's picture of perfection. We begin to frown on ourselves, and then we start to beat ourselves up internally because we don't fit the so called "mold". Well let me tell you something, you can look as good as you want to on the outside, but if your insides are all jacked up, you cannot do anything with your appearance accept walk around looking good with a bunch of turmoil within. Beauty is skin deep, but it is also in the eye of the beholder. The essence of who you are is simply amazing. It's time to embrace it!

Just as it is important to ensure that what we consume through our mouth, and allow into our system is good for us, don't you think that it is equally important that what we feed our psyche is good as well? This is why it is very, very, very important that we feed our psyche positively.

Emerge. Evolve. Transform. Transcend.

THE PRECIOUS GEM COLLECTION

What we feed our psyche is so very important, because we will eventually emulate and reflect the state of the psyche. For this very reason, you must make it your business to affirm yourself daily. Positive affirmations promote wellness, increased self-esteem, healing, and confidence. It's self-performed therapy!

Gems, I want to share with you some ways of affirming yourself by way of spoken word. Remember, what you affirm, you reaffirm by putting into practice each day. Your affirmation should begin with the "I AM" statement, and should be in the present tense. What I have learned in my life is that you should never strive for something that is not attached to your God given purpose. You must first visualize yourself doing, being, and saying exactly what it is you desire, and then you must own it! No one can own it for you, you must own it yourself. You cannot give to others what you cannot give to yourself, and so it is pertinent that you start with self. The greatest form of affirmation is the Word of God. "FOR THE WORD OF GOD IS QUICK, AND POWERFUL, AND SHARPER THAN ANY TWO EDGED SWORD, PIERCING EVEN TO THE DIVIDING ASUNDER OF SOUL AND SPIRIT, AND OF THE JOINTS AND MARROW, AND IS A DISCERNER OF THE THOUGHTS AND INTENTS OF THE HEART" (Hebrews 4:12-KJV). "I CAN DO ALL THINGS THROUGH CHRIST WHO STRENGTHENS ME" (Philippians 4:13-KJV). "YE ARE OF GOD, LITTLE CHILDREN, AND HAVE OVERCOME THEM:
BECAUSE GREATER IS HE THAT IS IN YOU, THAN HE THAT IS IN THE WORLD" (1 John 4:4-KJV). "NO WEAPON THAT IS FORMED AGAINST THEE SHALL PROSPER;" (Isaiah 54:17-KJV). "FOR THE JOY OF THE LORD IS YOUR STRENGTH" (Nehemiah 8:10-KJV).

THE PRECIOUS GEM COLLECTION

Here are a few examples of what I utilize to keep myself moving forward in a positive direction: I AM STRONG! I AM WELL ABLE TO FULFILL MY DESTINY IN CHRIST! I AM SUCCESSFUL! I AM CAPABLE! I AM PATIENT! I AM COURAGEOUS! I AM HIGHLY FAVORED BY THE LORD! I AM CREATIVE! I AM BRILLIANT! I AM BEAUTIFUL! I AM AN OVERCOMER! I AM APPROVED! I AM A WINNER! I AM A SURVIVOR! I AM MORE THAN A CONQUEROR! I AM A CHILD OF GOD, WISE, GUIDED AND LOVED!

It is so very easy for us as human beings to fill our thoughts with negativity, and due to the fact that we do consume a lot of what we hear, it is very important that we make sure we counteract negative consumption and negative thinking with positive consumption and positive thinking. Do what is necessary to rid your mind, body and soul of negativity. "And be not conformed to this world: but be ye transformed by the renewing of your mind, that ye may prove what is that good, and acceptable, and perfect, will of God" (Romans 12:2-KJV). Surround yourself with positive people who lift and not always lean. Fill your living space with inspiration and things that stimulate positivity. It is important to keep a fresh vision, for lack of vision breeds a futile existence.

Keep Striving! Keep Dreaming! Keep Creating! Keep Being!

THE PRECIOUS GEM COLLECTION

GIVE IT TO GOD

So often we cast our cares on the Lord and give our burdens over to Him because they are too much for us to carry. However, the first chance we get, we take it back and try to rewrite the script that He has so perfectly scripted from the beginning. We rehearse our pain by either revisiting it frequently, or by meditating on the pain we felt before we released our cares and placed them in the hands of the Lord. We fail to realize that if the same pains, worries, doubts, and fears that held us captive for so long were truly left in God's hands, we really would not suffer such anguish when reminiscing on them. It's a new season, and it's time that we truly let go and let God, for it is unto Him who is able to do immeasurably more than we could ever ask or imagine according to His power that is at work within us. Do not hold on to the wrong things people have done to you. Let go of the anger and bitter feelings that fester in your heart and cause your spirit to be disrupted. Forgive those who trespass against you because God has forgiven each of us our sins. "As far as the east is from the west, so far hath he removed our transgressions from us." (Psalm 103:12-KJV) If folk knew better, they would most certainly do better. And, that is why we cannot hold it against another human being when they falter or fail us. We are fearfully and wonderfully made in Christ, and while the element of imperfection still exists because we are human, we must allow our flesh to decrease and our spirit to increase so that God may be glorified.

There may be times when you want to take it to the streets on someone and tell them off in every language because they did you wrong. However, you must ask yourself what the noble thing would be to do. It is best to turn the other cheek, and that is exactly what we must do in situations where we have fallen prey to someone else's insensitivity. People can be cruel, cold, and harsh, but I have learned that there is a root to every problem. Sometimes people hurt you intentionally or unintentionally because they are in pain, and they may not even be aware of it.

THE PRECIOUS GEM COLLECTION

The pain they carry might seep through the core of their existence and affect you, and then you are the one left feeling targeted and abused. Everyone has issues, whether they are bold enough to admit it or not. Some do a good job of dressing them up, and others wear them right on their sleeve. Whatever the case may be, issues are meant to be dealt with. And, sometimes we may be the only sign of light that people receive. For this very reason, it is pertinent that we put on the full armor of God so that we may stand strong, armed and ready to release a positive word that will deflect negativity when it comes our way.

There will always be fires to put out because we live in world filled with so much evil. However, we also know that love covers a multitude of sins. In order to be victorious, we must deflect hatred with love. Stand firm and know that God fights your battles daily. You are more than conquerors! "Casting all your care upon him; for he careth for you…But the God of all grace, who hath called us unto his eternal glory by Christ Jesus, after that ye have suffered a while, make you perfect, establish, strengthen, settle you. To him be glory and dominion for ever and ever. Amen." (1 Peter 5:7-KJV)

THE PRECIOUS GEM COLLECTION

RARE & PRECIOUS JEWELS

Did you know that you were all rare and precious jewels? If not, let me just remind you of how precious, rare, unique and special you are. Just as DNA is unique to every individual, your character and personality are all yours and absolutely no one can take your place. There is nobody on earth exactly like you, and that is why you have the right to celebrate precious YOU. So Precious Gems, the next time you look at a beautiful diamond or a precious stone, salute yourself because you fall into that same category. You are a child of God, wise, guided and loved. And in case no one told you today, you are beautiful and special in every single way!

THE PRECIOUS GEM COLLECTION

WHAT DREAMS ARE MADE OF

So often in life, we hope, we dream, and we wish for things. We wait for the magical day when all of our dreams will become a reality. We fail to realize that God is the author of life. He holds the Master Plan in His hand, for He is the potter and we are the clay. There comes a point in one's life when dreams are no longer sought after, but rather attainable as they manifest through our purpose. Dreams can become reality and hope does not have to be fleeting. However, for everything that you aspire to achieve, there is a process that has to take place in order for you to receive the promise.

It may seem as if the process is long and drawn out at times, or that progress is way off in the distance. We tend to have this picture in our heads of how things ought to be, and how things will be when our dreams come true. However, we never really know how things will unfold exactly. God holds the blueprint for our lives, and while we may hold certain pieces to the puzzle, He is the One who will complete it. "Being confident of this very thing, that he which hath begun a good work in you will perform it until the day of Jesus: Even as it is meet for me to think this of you all, because I have you in my heart; inasmuch as both in my bonds, and in the defense and confirmation of the gospel, ye all are partakers of my grace." (Philippians 1:6-KJV) We take certain measures to fulfill our dream with the notion that our way is the best way, or that there is only one way to reach a certain aspiration. What I have come to realize, is that if you delight yourself in the Lord, He will certainly grant you the desires of your heart. Now one might say that it is virtually impossible to follow a blueprint that is faith based when we live in a world that is based on and often promotes the "gotta see it to believe it" philosophy.

In the Word it says to walk by faith and not by sight. It also states to seek ye first the kingdom of God and His righteousness; and all these things shall be added unto you. (Matthew 6:33-KJV)

THE PRECIOUS GEM COLLECTION

If you believe it, then you can achieve it! There is nothing that God does not order that He does not prepare you for. The steps of a righteous man are ordered by the Lord. "For I know the thoughts that I think toward you, saith the LORD, thoughts of peace, and not of evil, to give you an expected end." (Jeremiah 29:11-KJV) It is best to surrender your will and submit to His will, for ultimately His *will* be done. The road may be hard at times, and you may even get lost along the way, but the Lord is your shepherd and He will guide you on your way. He will always lead you to the place where you belong. His purpose for your life is in perfect alignment with His perfect plan and will for your life. He sometimes takes you the long way so that He can instill some things in you that would not otherwise be captured if He took you on the short route.

God wants His children to maintain and be sustained in the fulfillment of His promise. He does not want us to get to a certain destination without the ability to withstand it. For this reason, we must go through seasons of preparation and drought so that we are well equipped rather than ill equipped. "Therefore I say unto you, Take no thought for your life, what ye shall eat, or what ye shall drink; nor yet for your body, what ye shall put on..."(Matthew 6:25-34-KJV) He said that He would supply all of our needs according to His riches in Heaven. (Philippians 4:19-NIV) You are empowered to prosper!

THE PRECIOUS GEM COLLECTION

COME IN OUT OF THE RAIN

Whenever I am in the midst of a storm and I seek the face of the Lord, I am quickly reminded that this too shall pass. When we go to our Heavenly Father to summon His hand and ask for wisdom, He also adds understanding. His thoughts and His ways are higher than our thoughts and our ways. For this very reason, He instructs us to "Trust in the Lord with all thine heart; and lean not unto thine own understanding. In all thy ways acknowledge him, and he shall direct thy paths." (Proverbs 3:5-6-KJV)

It is not always easy to place His Word higher than our thoughts because as humans we want to rely on our natural mind. However, we must rely on His Word, for it is an infallible truth that we can stand firmly upon. I have also learned that the Lord has granted us earthly beings such as the family and friends that serve as a support system for us when we stand in the face of a storm. Whenever I seek the counsel of my dad, he always reminds me that "calms seas do not make a skillful sailor, for it is by raging waters and turbulent storms that a sailor can be made skillful."

Whenever I seek the counsel of my mom, she always tells me to "be still and slow to speak, for everything will work out for your good." These statements bring to my remembrance the scripture in Mark 4:37-39 which states: "And there arose a great storm of wind, and the waves beat into the ship, so that it was now full. And he was in the hinder part of the ship, asleep on a pillow: and they awake him, and say unto him, Master, carest thou not that we perish? And he arose, and rebuked the wind, and said unto the sea, 'Peace, be still.' And the wind ceased, and there was a great calm." (KJV) This scripture denotes peace in the midst of a turbulent storm that would have otherwise killed them if Jesus did not speak to the raging waters. He taught His disciples a major lesson while in the midst of what seemed to be a hopeless situation, a lesson of faith.

THE PRECIOUS GEM COLLECTION

"And he said unto them, Why are ye so fearful? how is it that ye have no faith? And they feared exceedingly, and said one to another, What manner of man is this, that even the wind and the sea obey him?" (Mark 4:40&41-KJV)

What God wants is for us to trust Him at *all* times, even in the midst of a violent storm. He wants us to have faith that He will always go before us to prepare the way that He has set for us. Even when the winds and waters are raging and it seems like there is no shield from the rain, God will serve as our indestructible shield and covering. He will stand for us when we are weak. He will speak to our situations even when we lack the faith, for even when we are faithless, God *remains* faithful.

"He that dwelleth in the secret place of the most High shall abide under the shadow of the Almighty. I will say of the LORD, He is my refuge and my fortress: my God; in him will I trust. Surely he shall deliver thee from the snare of the fowler, and from the noisome pestilence. He shall cover thee with his feathers, and under his wings shalt thou trust: his truth shall be thy shield and buckler." (Psalms 91:1-4-KJV)

THE PRECIOUS GEM COLLECTION

CHAPTER 3

***

TRANSFORM

Emerge. Evolve. Transform. Transcend.

THE PRECIOUS GEM COLLECTION

FORGET THE PAST

"Forgetting what is behind and straining toward what is ahead, I press on toward what is ahead, I press on toward the goal to win the prize for which God has called me heavenward in Christ Jesus." (Philippians 3:13, 14-NIV)

So often in life we try to hold on so tightly to our past. By doing so, we are stagnated and prevented from moving forward. We hold onto past mistakes and failures, allowing them to be our cushion, when all the while we should effort to free ourselves of the past. We hold tightly to the fear, pain and regret associated with our past. We become haunted by the things of the past, so much so, that we tend to dwell in a space that leaves little to no room for growth, healing or progress. We hold on to the notion that we could have, should have or would have done better in the past. Also, if given the chance, we would travel back in time to relive, fix or change the things that we feel should have been different. However, we must realize that "For those God foreknew he also predestined to be conformed to the likeness of his Son, that he might be the firstborn among many brothers. And those he predestined, he also called; those he called, he also justified; those he justified, he also glorified."(Romans 8:29&30- KJV) God knows the end from the beginning, for He is the Alpha and the Omega. "Before I formed you in the womb I knew you, before you were born I set you apart…" (Jeremiah 1:5-NIV)

We must realize that yesterday is gone, and the only way the pain from our past can truly affect us in the present day, is if we allow it to. We give more power to those things that are negative and that will only cause us to suffer, rather than holding firm to the power and love that God freely gives us. His mercy endures forever and His grace is sufficient. We cannot change the past, but we can live for today and lay the foundation for a better future.

THE PRECIOUS GEM COLLECTION

"For I know the plans I have for you," declares the LORD , "plans to prosper you and not to harm you, plans to give you hope and a future."(Jeremiah 29:1-NIV)

THE PRECIOUS GEM COLLECTION

GET UP! GET OUT! DO SOMETHING!

Waking up with breath of life every morning is a gift granted. However, getting out of bed is a choice that we make. Sometimes it may seem as if getting out of bed is the hardest thing to do, especially when you are going through something difficult. However, I am here to tell you that all you have to do is take the first step and allow God to do the rest. It is always easier to wallow in your pain while facing trials and tribulation. It is also easy to throw yourself a pity party and invite all those who will allow you stay in a ditch full of sorrow. However, you should endeavor to do just the opposite, by surrounding yourself with positive people who not only love you, but who will also support you in your time of need.

Prayers, encouragement, motivation, and inspiration go a mighty long way, and you would be surprised how far love can take you. The key to surviving any trial is to focus on the solution rather than the problem at hand. God will definitely see you through, and He will equip you with necessary tools that will enable you to get up, get out, and do something! You don't have to stay down in the dumps, nor do you have to swim in your own sorrow. There is a season for everything under the sun, and no matter the season, God will see you through. Be it happy or sad, up or down, left or right, small or large, rain or shine, day or night, God is in control. He will always make a way for you to endure and overcome every obstacle. The battle is not yours, simply be still and He will fight for you. (Exodus 14:14-NIV)

Celebrate your life and throw a VICTORY party, for you are more than a conqueror!

THE PRECIOUS GEM COLLECTION

IGNITE THE FIRE WITHIN

The worth of an individual cannot be measured, for the capacity is too great. Taking pride in yourself is highly recommended, for if you value yourself, you then pave the way for others to respect you. In order for one to command respect, one must first respect himself and give the same respect one desires in return. One cannot expect from others what they do not believe they deserve and/or can provide. We tend to be a huge reflection of whom or what we encounter in life. Have you ever pondered why you may attract certain individuals, or why the same behaviors that you do not want to acknowledge in yourself are being exhibited by someone else? Are you left feeling a sense of frustration, disgust, and resentment? Now do not get me wrong Gems, we have all encountered things that in no way, shape or form reflect who we are, or what we aspire to become. However, we must take inventory of the things that we do come into contact with, because there is most often a lesson to be learned.

So often individuals walk around demanding respect, but they do not want to give it. So many individuals walk around searching for validation from others, but they must first understand that validation comes first from oneself. We were all created with flaws and imperfections, but we are also fearfully and wonderfully made. Whether it is the physical, mental, emotional, or spiritual, we must embrace every aspect of who we are. Once we accept and embrace the very essence of who we are, we will then be able to grow and walk in the fullness of who God created us to be. God is the potter and we are the clay. He will continue to mold, form, and shape our character, as He has carefully crafted our lives. Now of course we all want to play the part by looking and acting a certain way. However, the clothes, the car, the house, and the jewels don't make the individual, for it is the heart of an individual that makes them shine. For this reason, the statement "You are what you eat" can be broken down in many different ways.

THE PRECIOUS GEM COLLECTION

Whatever you allow into your system will most often play out if you do not take inventory of the things you consume. Whether it is by surrounding yourself with and/or modeling your life after certain entities, we are all susceptible to being influenced by either positive or negative forces. If we constantly allow negative thoughts to enter into our minds, we will most often replay those negative thoughts and they will consume us. If we allow people to speak negatively to us, and if we never surround ourselves with positive people who can feed us in a positive manner, we will most often form the habit of speaking negatively of ourselves and others.

Positive energy incites positive energy. Negative energy fuels negative energy; and it only stirs up confusion. All it takes is a single strike of a match to ignite a fire, and all it takes is a single positive word, thought or action to ignite a positive attitude. Don't allow anyone to fuel a negative fire in you. by striking a negative match. You have the power to ignite a positive fire within yourself. Laughter, love, joy and peace are contagious, and all it takes is one person to create a snowball effect. Surround yourself with positive energy, and positive energy will eventually grow and expand into a huge mass of positive energy that will engulf your life in entirety.

"I will praise You, for I am fearfully and wonderfully made..."~(Psalms139:14-NIV)

THE PRECIOUS GEM COLLECTION

PEACE BE STILL!

When you take the time to listen and be still, not only do you open yourself up to learn more, but you avail yourself to the things that would not be accessible to you unless you were still. You begin to hear things that you would not ordinarily hear, and often times it will seem like an angel whispered softly in your ear. There are also life messages floating around everywhere, and there is always a message waiting to be spoken into your heart. A lot of times, we as human beings spend more time talking and doing, rather than simply being still.

There is a lot to say about being still, because it is during those quiet moments when you hear the messages that are being spoken softly to your heart. It is during those moments of solace when many answers come. It is during those moments of solitude when direction and guidance are given.

So often we look outside of ourselves for the answers that we are in search of. However, what we fail to realize is that the answer lies within us. The very essence of who we are as human beings is precious, and we must nurture that essence. The necessities of life consist of food, clothing, and shelter, but we must remember that replenishment is the necessity of the soul. We neglect to retreat and clear out the clutter that resides within the crevices of our core. We neglect to quiet the endless chatter in our minds and rest. We stray so far away from meditation and prayer, the entities that enable us to really hear from God. Each entity in itself provides healing and nourishment for the mind, body, and soul. We are empowered to acquiesce in a place of peace and restoration, even when everything around us does not comply. We must exercise our faith and hold firm to the truths that allow us to embrace whatever messages that are meant for us to receive.

BE STILL…There is a message waiting for you, open up and let it in!

THE PRECIOUS GEM COLLECTION

REDEMPTION THROUGH CHRIST

We were born into this world with a sinful nature, and even though we all struggle with sin, we shall not allow it to have a foothold. "For God so loved the world that he gave his one and only Son, that whoever believes in him shall not perish but have eternal life."(John 3:16-NIV) God sent His Son Jesus Christ to grant us all salvation and his intention was not to condemn us, but to redeem us. "For all have sinned and fall short of the glory of God, and are justified freely by his grace through the redemption that came by Christ Jesus." (Romans 3:23&24-NIV) Jesus, who sits at the right hand of God, intercedes for us so that we may have peace with God. For Christ who died on the cross for our sins while we were yet sinners, has given us eternal life and because of Him we are able to go to God and ask for forgiveness. "This is the covenant I will make with them after that time, says the Lord. I will put my laws in their hearts, and I will write them on their minds. Then he adds: 'Their sins and lawless acts I will remember no more.' And where these have been forgiven, there is no longer any sacrifice for sin. Therefore, brothers, since we have confidence to enter the Most Holy Place by the blood of Jesus, by a new and living way opened for us through the curtain, that is, his body, and since we have a great priest over the house of God, let us draw near to God with a sincere heart in full assurance of faith, having our hearts sprinkled to cleanse us from a guilty conscience and having our bodies washed with pure water." (Hebrews 10:15-22-NIV) We are fearfully and wonderfully made in Christ. In Christ, old things are passed away and we are made new. Through Christ, redemption is granted and forgiveness is given. Open up your heart and let Him in, He loves you and He will welcome you with open arms.

THE PRECIOUS GEM COLLECTION

THAT SPECIAL SOMEONE

Loving yourself is the greatest gift that you could give to yourself and to others, because when you love yourself, you make room for others to love you just the same.

For all of you who are waiting for that special someone to enter into your life, always remember that a special someone is waiting for you too. When that special someone arrives, you will recognize them because they will be a reflection of who you are, and they will mirror the love that you have for yourself and much more. They will have your best interest at heart, and they will allow you to grow in a positive direction. They will accept you for who you are, and they will only encourage you to make positive changes. Never will they try to alter you in a way that forces you to lose your sense of self or self-worth. However, they will work together with you to mesh those qualities that you both possess into a beautiful, loving, and healthy relationship. You will be the apple of their eye, and they will cherish all that you are. They will hold your heart and handle it with extreme care, like that of a precious and rare jewel. They will cherish the treasure that they found in you.

Be still, your special someone is on the way and they are tailor made just for you!

THE PRECIOUS GEM COLLECTION

THE SEAT OF CONSCIOUSNESS

It is not always easy to practice what you preach, but I have learned that to teach is to learn twice.

There are so many hidden channels within all of us, and we all possess an enormous capacity to retain information. The brain is utterly amazing! The capacity of the mind is enormous, as it enables us to retain and store more content than we could possibly imagine. To sit high on the seat of consciousness is an amazing and powerful thing. The conscious mind is a playground. If we learn to channel our positive thoughts and energy, our creative pursuits would become increasingly productive.

We all have dreams to seek and goals that we would like to achieve in this life; and the great thing is that we are all capable beings. As long as we are willing in the pursuit of our endeavors, we can accomplish anything we put our minds to.

If you can perceive it Gems, then you most certainly can achieve it!

THE PRECIOUS GEM COLLECTION

TIME

Time reveals all things. Whatever sits in the seat of your soul will come forth at the right time. If we all took a moment to reflect on our past and our present state, we would see a huge distinction between the two. The past and the present each serve a major purpose, because they lay the foundation for our future. Making the transition from childhood to adulthood is something that we have all had to endure, and it may not have always been easy. However, we can attribute a lot of who we are today to that transition. I am sure that we have all experienced growing pains, the times in which we were really discovering our own identity, growing into our own personalities, developing our own thoughts, and formulating our own opinions. That was a time when we began to see the big picture and everything seemed to be magnified. Our minds can encompass more than we could ever imagine. As children we are able to live care-free lives, but as adults we are confronted with reality. We are faced with a lot more challenges and responsibility. As adults we are accountable for ourselves. We are held accountable for our own actions and sometimes the actions of others, especially if one holds the responsibility of being a guardian or care-taker. The transition is indeed a beautiful one, because it grants us an opportunity to grow, transform and evolve. There are many stages involved in the transitional process, but the beauty of it all, is that life does accommodate us along the way.

Imagine if everything were thrown at us all at once, especially at a time when we were not prepared to receive it and could not handle it. We would be overwhelmed and under extreme pressure. It's just like when you were a child and you asked your parents for a particular toy or accessory that you very much desired. I am sure that there have been times when your parents said "NO!" You may have responded with the infamous question "WHY?" and they may have responded to that question by saying, "I am your parent, I love you, and I know what is best for you."

THE PRECIOUS GEM COLLECTION

Perhaps you were not ready for what you asked your parents for, and could not see the big picture at the time. All you may have heard was the answer "NO!" and you were probably extremely disappointed. Well Gems, it's the same way with God and our lives. Can you think of a couple of things that you may have prayed and asked God for? Did you always receive those things on your timetable and in the manner in which you thought you would receive it? Speaking on my own behalf, I can honestly say that I have not always received answered prayers in the manner in which I expected, but they are always answered according to God's perfect plan and will for my life. I have learned to pray that God's will be done in my life, and that I stand in perfect alignment with His will. Now I am not saying that it is always easy, for I am human and do want my way sometimes. However, I have learned that it is best to just surrender to His will. He is abounding in love and His mercy endures forever. God knows what is best for us, and He not only takes into account our past and present, but He sees much farther ahead into our future.

"For I know the plans I have for you," declares the Lord, "plans to prosper you and not to harm you, plans to give you hope and a future." (Jeremiah 29:11-13-NIV) He weaves our past, present and future into the equation of our lives and He sees fit to put His plan in order because He loves us and does want the very best for us. Don't be discouraged when things do not go the way that you planned or expected Gems, because God's timing is impeccable and He is always on time. His thoughts and His ways are higher than our thoughts and our ways. "As for God, his way is perfect; the word of the Lord is flawless." (2 Samuel 22:31-NIV)

God has your life in the palm of His mighty hand Precious Gems, and everything is in divine order!

THE PRECIOUS GEM COLLECTION

VICTORIOUS!

Are you a rose amidst a field of piercing thorns?
Are you a honeycomb amidst a swarm of violent bees?
Are you a sheep amidst a pack of hungry wolves?
Are you an antelope being sought by a vicious lion?

Have you fallen prey to the attacks of humankind? Do you feel like you stand alone with no chance of gaining the victory over your situation? Are you preparing for defeat, rather than victory? Are you rebelling against the purpose for your life instead of surrendering to God's perfect plan and will for your life? If so Gems, please surrender and let God fight this battle for you. The battle is not yours, it's the Lord's!

We live in a harsh and cruel world, where the pangs of life try so hard to beat us down and tear us apart. However, we have access to a higher power that is *always* available to us. God is ready and willing to come to our aid when necessary, for He is a very present help in times of trouble. All we have to do is summon the power of Almighty God that lies within us and we can win a battle that seems futile. All that we need to survive resides on the inside of us, for greater is He that is in us. Assume the position in this fight of faith and put on the full armor of God. We must continue to stand and fight, walk by faith and not by sight.

The VICTORY is yours, for the battle has already been won. You are more than a conqueror!

THE PRECIOUS GEM COLLECTION

WAIT ON THE LORD!

"Wait on the Lord; be of good courage, and He shall strengthen your heart; wait, I say, on the Lord!" (Psalm 27:14-NIV)

Has there ever been a time in your life when you felt as though you were in a waiting area, waiting on the Lord to show up and show out? You may have had a long list of things that you needed and desired of the Lord, and you may have felt like He abandoned you. Well Gems, I am here to tell you that while you may feel like you have been waiting forever for the Lord to show up, please believe that He is ever present and His timing is impeccable! He has an anointed and appointed time for everything under the sun, and for everything there is a season. "There is a time for everything, and a season for every activity under heaven." (Ecclesiastes 3:1-NIV)

You may be waiting on DELIVERANCE, JOY, LOVE, PEACE, HEALING, STRENGTH, WISDOM, UNDERSTANDING, JUSTICE, PROMISES, A MATE, FINANCES, REVELATION, CONFIRMATION, ANSWERS, EMPLOYMENT, A HOME, A CAR, A WORD, A CHILD or simply CHANGE. I am here to tell you that whatever you want, God's got it! It's all in Him Gems, so wait on Him to call your name, and be careful to give Him all the Glory when He does. He is worthy. Hold on my Gems, a change is coming at God's appointed time!

"Those who hope in the Lord will renew their strength. They will soar on wings like eagles; they will run and not grow weary, they will walk and not be faint." (Isaiah 40:31-NIV)

THE PRECIOUS GEM COLLECTION

WHEN YOU'VE DONE ALL YOU CAN

What do you do when you have done all that you can? You must STAND!

Through all of life's ups and downs, God remains the same. He is the same yesterday, today, and forever. From the moment you were brought into the world you were susceptible to all kinds of challenges and fiery darts. However, there is a name above every name that overcame the world on your behalf, and He continues to fight our battles daily. His name is Jesus Christ. "For God so loved the world that He gave His only begotten Son, that whoever believes in Him should not perish but have everlasting life." (John 3:16-NIV) What this verse exemplifies is VICTORY!!! We are more than conquerors in Christ. "No weapon formed against you shall prosper." (Isaiah 54:7-NIV)

There may be times when you feel like you have walked into a crossfire of chaos and destruction. However, do not fear, for you are never alone. "As for God, His way is perfect; the word of the Lord is flawless. He is a shield for all who take refuge in Him."(2 Samuel 22:31-NIV) God is allowing His perfect plan and will for your life to unfold. "For I know the plans I have for you," declares the Lord, "plans to prosper you and not to harm you, plans to give you hope and a future."(Jeremiah 29:11-NIV) No one said that the road would be easy, but I guarantee you that God did not bring you this far to leave you. He has a wonderful, mighty and awesome plan in store for your life, all He wants you to do is trust Him.

"As the rain and the snow come down from heaven, and do not return to it without watering the earth and making it bud and flourish, so that it yields seed for the sower and bread for the eater, so is my word that goes out from my mouth: It will not return to me empty, but will accomplish what I desire and achieve the purpose for which I sent it." (Isaiah 55:10-NIV) "The grass withers and the flowers fall, but the word of our God stands forever."(Isaiah 40:8-NIV)

THE PRECIOUS GEM COLLECTION

So when dark clouds form over your life, and the rain starts pouring down, don't lose faith and give up hope Gems, simply stand and fight!

When your finances have crashed, STAND!
When your heart is broken, STAND!
When your job brings you misery, STAND!
When your friends turn their backs on you, STAND!
When your family is torn apart, STAND!
When your relationship is in a disarray, STAND!
When things just aren't going your way, STAND!

THE PRECIOUS GEM COLLECTION

LIFE LESSONS

One never realizes just how much their presence affects the life of another until they are absent. I want to share with you some of the lessons I have learned over the years; I am sure that they will be a great asset to you, if not now, maybe later.

First, I learned just how deep, far and wide strength really goes. I learned that in your weakest state, you are really at your strongest. Moreover, at what appears to be your lowest point, you are actually in a good place. You become a candidate for a miracle move of God. Your faith is really put to the test and fortified when you are at your lowest point. I learned to stop, look and listen to what is going on in and around me during a trial. At your lowest point is usually when the universe can really go to work, revealing answers to questions held deep within, as well as things that are hidden from your sight. You definitely do learn who your friends are in the midst of adversity, for it is so easy to be there for someone when life is a breeze, but when life takes you on a turbulent ride, friends will either stay by your side or flee the scene.

Second, I learned that all that glitters is definitely not gold, no matter how beautifully wrapped it is. The heart of a human being is where the true treasure lies. Never let appearances deceive you. Be slow to speak and quick to hear, for people will most often tell you who they are as soon as they open their mouths. Trust your gut instinct always, for it will never steer you wrong. Be real with yourself, and always *be* yourself, it will cause people to either step up or step off if they are running game. What's done in the dark will most definitely be brought to the light, so you do not have to worry about people getting away with the evil they do against you in secret. What goes around comes back around. What you put out comes back to you; it's the law of the universe. Never wish harm on anyone, for the same harm you wish could quite possibly come back to you. Leave it in God's hands, for vengeance is His. He will definitely take care of it. Believe in yourself, and know who you are. Stand for something, because if you stand for nothing, you will fall for everything. Stay away from darkness, and always stand in

THE PRECIOUS GEM COLLECTION

the light.

    Third, always turn trials into treasure. What you cannot fix, you should always improve. Find a positive outlet for stress, anger, frustration, and pain. Use your gifts and do not let them fall away. Perfect your craft and put it to good use. Ask for help when needed. Surround yourself with positive people that will push you towards your goals and to pursue your dreams. Try to stay away from people who always lean but rarely lift. When in a barrel full of crabs, always stay on top so that you are closest to the exit and not drawn towards the bottom where you run the risk of becoming like those trying to pull you down. Sharpen your skills while in the midst of a trial. Learn the lessons that your trials are supposed to teach you. Be ready for your test at the end of the trial, because most often the same questions will appear that were on your last test. Remember all that you learned in your past season of trials and you will pass the test with flying colors. Never forget that you are more than a conqueror and you *cannot* lose. If God be for you, who can be against you? The key is to never stop moving forward.

    People enter into our lives for a reason, a season, or a lifetime. They are there to either fulfill a purpose, help you get to a certain destination, be your support during a rough time, help you to emerge and unveil a part of you that was hidden deep behind fear, teach you something that you need to learn, or may simply be an answer to prayer. It's hard for most people to understand sheer generosity and altruism because so many people have hidden agendas. No one seems to believe that good deeds can be done without expectations and no strings attached. This is the reason why people get hurt or end up confused. Their motives are out of whack. People hold so tightly to things that will give them a definite link to someone, failing to realize that you can't lose what's yours, nor can you lose something you never had in the first place. We must remain in daily pursuit of acceptance, in order to come to grips with the very things we cannot change or control.

THE PRECIOUS GEM COLLECTION

In life, we will be faced with many challenges, and there will be things that we may not always understand. However, we must accept them and move on. We cannot figure out God's next move, and if we could, then it would take away from our growth and dependence on Him and His sovereignty. God is in control. Everything is in divine order; everything happens at the divine and appointed time, be it good or bad. We must not fret over the things we have no control over, because it is out of our hands. We must take life one day at a time and cherish each moment as if it were our last. Do not worry about tomorrow because tomorrow has worries of its own. Be still and take each moment one step at a time. All things work together for good, and if you just trust in the Lord and have faith, you will reach your destination in peace.

THE PRECIOUS GEM COLLECTION

LOVE THYSELF!

We live in a society that is so obsessed with beauty and perfection, so much so that we pursue it at all costs. We look in magazines and watch the latest shows in order to keep updated on the latest trends in fashion and beauty, failing to realize that beauty is only skin deep. We look so hard to find a glimpse of ourselves in models, actors/actresses and all of the latest gear. However, we fail to look for the beauty that resides within the soul. We go under the knife and await the cut that we believe will dramatically alter our appearance and transform our existence, when we really need to alter our perception of self. We are so unhappy with the bodies we are born with and the characteristics that are part of our genetic make-up, so much so, that we take drastic measures in order to change it, even if it means endangering our own well-being. However, until we learn that it is not the physical appearance that defines us, we will not be able to love the skin that we are in. We all are made up of tiny imperfections, and that's what makes us human. There are some things that I am sure we can all afford to change on the outside, but does that really change who we are on the inside? We hold onto the notion that increased confidence and self- esteem may come along with the appearance of perfection, but what happens when we discover yet another flaw? We embark on a never ending journey trying to become satisfaction-seekers, always looking for our next quick fix, failing to realize that we are beautiful just the way we are!

The soul of an individual goes deeper than the surface of their physical being. The character of an individual is not reflected in what one wears, but more significantly in what they say and do. The heart of an individual is where the true treasure lies, for there resides the wellspring of life. Love yourself Gems and cherish the skin you're in. You're beautiful!

THE PRECIOUS GEM COLLECTION

HEAL THYSELF!

God knows exactly where you are and can meet you right where you stand. However, sometimes you must leave where you are to hear His voice. I recently ventured off to Los Angeles for a brief vacation, to get away from the hustle and bustle of New York City. What I recently learned will carry me through life as I move forward on my journey of self-discovery, and I hope it will do the same for you. I learned that balance is as essential to our living, thriving and survival as the air we breathe. It is pertinent for any human being to manage their time and energy wisely, or else you will find that you are offline and out of tune with the rest of the universe.

One must not give his time and energy away to any and everybody, because not everyone is deserving of it. I find that people often pull me in many different directions, be it family, friends, colleagues, and sometimes even complete strangers. I am bound to be taken on a rollercoaster ride if I allow myself to. I was recently feeling drained and overwhelmed, but I could not pin point exactly where my lack of energy derived from, not until I broke away from my environment. I was so bombarded by phones calls, visits, overwhelming demands and life in general. My vision began to blur, my thoughts became obscured, and my physical well-being was literally at stake. My body was tired. I was not eating right, nor was I eating on a consistent basis. I was cranky and I began to lose a level head. This is when I realized that I needed to escape for a little while in an effort to restore my soul. I needed to be free from any and every distraction, and I needed to flee to a place where I could free my mind. I chose to spend a day at the beach, and this is where I found momentary solace. One must slip away to find a quiet place to quiet their mind, collect their thoughts, and simply relax. People will pull at you as long as you allow them to, but you must be like a tree firmly planted. This is when learning to balance comes into play.

THE PRECIOUS GEM COLLECTION

People tend to pull at you when they feel they are deficient in one or more areas where you are sufficient, all the while they may be blind to the fact that you still need to replenish yourself in order to give of yourself. They leach on to you and zap you of any strength you have, leaving you with little to no room for healthy growth or improvement. While you are busy trying to *do* all and *be* all to everybody, you fail to take the necessary time out to replenish, rejuvenate, and restore yourself. You won't be able to think straight if you continue on this path. Your internal clock will be thrown off. Your eating habits will become poor, and your sleep patterns will be totally out of whack. It is okay to put things on hold for a day or two, your well-being comes first! We get so caught up in the day-to-day affairs of life that we tend to forget about ourselves. We are so afraid to shut the door, unplug the phone, and turn off the lights on the world for a moment. We hold on to the notion that if we don't do it, it won't get done, or that if we step away for a moment, everything will fall apart. Newsflash Gems! Everything is in divine order, and will fall into place the way it's supposed to. Take the time to heal yourself. You'll be better off, and you'll have much more to give. Balance is essential!

THE PRECIOUS GEM COLLECTION

LEARN TO SAY NO!

"NO!" is such a powerful statement, and when we actually learn to use it, we are empowered! How many times has something been asked of you that really was not feasible for you at the time or simply impossible, but somehow you managed to say yes? I am sure that we have all been there at one time or another, and there are many reasons why "yes" may be able to roll of the tongue so easily in place of the word no.

One reason for this is because by default, human beings want to please one another on some level or another. We want to be there for each other by any means necessary. We want to follow through and make it happen for those that we love and care about. We want to make a good impression. It is in our nature to want to be all that we can be and much more. We love to go above and beyond the call of duty. We love to have a good reputation. We like to be looked up to and admired. We simply want to leave behind a legacy of good. We all want a good report!

Well Gems, I'm sorry to break the news to you, but we may have to let down, disappoint and perhaps even anger a few individuals in this life. Not everything is in our hands, within our reach, or possible to carry out. The problem does not lie in the "yes" itself, it lies in the behavior it is associated with. By you bending over backwards to get something done to please someone else, knowing full well that it is not possible for you, you run the risk of creating havoc for all parties involved. You open the door for heavy disappointment, and then you are not only seen as unreliable, but also rather dishonest. All the while, you could have prevented this turn of events by simply being honest and saying, "No, sorry I can't" or "I would love to, but it is just not in my means to do so." You then leave room for respect and trust, right along with your dignity being completely intact. One can always respect another for being honest. Honor the truth Gems, the truth will set you free, and it starts with you first being honest with yourself about what you can and cannot do.

THE PRECIOUS GEM COLLECTION

THE POWER OF FOCUS

When you make up in your mind to do something, there will always be distractions. This is when you must move forward with tunnel vision, allowing nothing or no one to get in your way. When you set your sights on something, focus your mind on a specific goal, and put it into action, everything around you is shaken up. However, if you stand your ground and keep pressing on, everything concerning you is forced to get in order. When you are focused, you tend to get things done quickly and accurately. There is power in focus, and the force behind you will continue to move you as long as you stay focused on forward progression. Lack of focus is a stumbling block in itself; it causes you to jump from one thing to the next, leaving things incomplete and undone. You are easily set back, and then you run the risk of becoming a procrastinator. You lose sight of what you want, and get frustrated when you see how far you could have gone if only you just stayed the course. It is not always easy to maintain focus, especially when life is full of distractions that seek to throw you off balance. Sometimes you have to fight to keep your focus, put your blinders on and hold your vision in plain view. At times it may be easier than others to focus, but it is an attainable feat. Use this life of yours, gifts and all. Hold your visions dear and run the race that is set before you with patience, endurance, and perseverance. The race is not given to the swift Gems, but to the one who can endure to the end. Focus on that goal, and hold firmly to that picture in your heart. You will reach your destination in peace.

Emerge. Evolve. Transform. Transcend.

THE PRECIOUS GEM COLLECTION

LET PEACE BE YOUR ANCHOR

Problems, yes they may come, but fret not! It is possible to have peace and the absence of anxiety in the midst of trouble. So often as human beings we have a tendency to worry about things we have no control over, especially tomorrow. Let's face it Gems, even though it's in our nature as human beings to worry at times, we must learn to try our best to accept the things we cannot change and do our best to change the things we can. We can easily get so used to having mayhem in our lives that when peace comes, we do away with it. We so easily forget that peace can reign in the midst. It's almost like we hold on to chaos like a security blanket, making it a necessary crutch. We forget that turmoil will only lead to internal destruction, because just as we are *"without"*, we are the same *"within"*. If you have made trouble your anchor in lieu of peace, it's time to switch it up. If you hold firm to the fact that nothing will happen to you that you and God together cannot handle, life will become a bit more peaceful for you. Fear, anxiety and worry are close cousins; they are peas in a pod. If you encounter one, you are bound to encounter the others. When they take residence in your life, you better believe that doubt and confusion are right around the corner laying a trap for you, causing you to lose faith, lack trust, and give up all hope. So often we allow fear, anxiety and worry to lead us, when they should be far off in the distance. Peace should always be in front, but we all know that it's hard gravitating towards peace when fear and worry have such a strong hold. You will know peace when it comes, for it is quiet and comforting. If ever you have had an encounter with peace, you know exactly what I am referring to. Most often peace will lead you in the right direction, guiding you towards what is good. There won't be any second guessing or annoying agitation in your spirit. Moving ahead without peace may often mean that you should wait for the right away, or stop because there is danger up ahead. This is when you need to stop, look, listen and wait for guidance and direction. Trust me when I tell you there have been many times when I wanted to move ahead into something, but I did not have peace

THE PRECIOUS GEM COLLECTION

about it. It could have been about anything, such as a purchase, employment, a transition, a relationship, or simply timing, but I have learned to follow peace, it never steers you wrong. Follow peace and let peace be your anchor. Let go of your worries about tomorrow or the future, take hold of the present moment and live your best life today. Storms may come, but as long as peace is your anchor, you will make it through the rain.

Let peace be your anchor today and all the days of your life. Be true to yourself and others, for it is you who has to live with YOU. Don't go against the current of life, simply ride the wave.

THE PRECIOUS GEM COLLECTION

ALL THINGS WORK TOGETHER FOR GOOD

Have you ever gone through a traumatic experience and thought to yourself, "How in the world am I ever going to get through this?" Well Gems, I am here to tell you that nothing negative happens to you that will not work out for your overall good. Do you not learn from everything you go through in life? Do you not come out stronger, wiser and much more audacious? Do you not grow as a result? Does your experience not serve as a stepping stone, testimony, and catalyst for someone else?

What does not kill you will only make you stronger. May you continue to grow through every experience Gems.

THE PRECIOUS GEM COLLECTION

DO WHAT YOU LOVE

Wherever you passion lies, there also lies your treasure. So many people walk around leading empty lives in search of something to make them complete. Not too many people are aware of the fact that joy lies deep within in a part of them that is waiting to be uncovered. If you have not discovered your passion, or found your niche in life, it's a good idea to start now. Yeah, you heard me Gems, RIGHT NOW! It's never too late to discover what you love. Guess what? It's usually right before your eyes, under your nose, in the palm of your hand, at the center of your heart, and a burning flame in your soul. It's already inside of you, and all you have to do is dig it up Gems. Start by asking yourself one simple question that will unlock the door to your passion. "What on earth do I like to do with my time and energy that brings me the most joy? What do I find myself doing during spare time that seems to make time fly by? What do I do well without having to put forth much effort? What natural talents do I possess?" These questions will aid you on your journey of self-discovery and unearthing your passion.

Unlock the treasure chest of your soul and dig up your passion, it lies within...

THE PRECIOUS GEM COLLECTION

GRATITUDE & PRAISE

How many times have you wanted to throw your hands up and throw in the towel on life, in addition to giving up on all that you strive for?

When the road of life gets tough, it's so easy to just quit and look at our situation from a pessimistic point of view. As soon as things get rough, we immediately start running off at the mouth, complaining about how hard it is to get by, how bad we have it, how much we lack, how far we have to go, and the list goes on. However, how often do we throw up our hands in gratitude and praise, thanking the Lord for all that we already have, how far we've already come, how He's already made a way out of no way, and the fact that we still have more life to live? Not often enough! I'm pretty sure that each and every one of us can think of one thing to be grateful for, and for that alone we should lift up our hands in praise. If the only thing that you can say is "Thank you," then so be it! Thank you goes a mighty long way Gems, as it is one of the greatest forms of gratitude known to man.

Stop Whining! Stop Complaining! Start Praising!

THE PRECIOUS GEM COLLECTION

WORTHY OF ALL THINGS GOOD

The manner in which you measure yourself is the same manner in which the world will measure you. If you love and respect yourself, you then cause others to do the same on your behalf. If you think lowly of yourself, you then grant others the right to look down upon you as well. You give people the power to either respect or disrespect you. In life, we have the power to teach everyone we encounter how to treat us. As human beings, it is our biggest tendency to expect from others what we can't even expect from ourselves. We want to be treated with respect, we want to be showered with love, we want, we want, we want, but do we give of ourselves exactly what we ask of others? It's a rarity!

Now don't get me wrong Gems, this does not excuse anyone from exercising fowl behavior, but it makes it that much more important that we treat ourselves and others with the same dignity and respect. We must first love ourselves before we can give love to someone else. We must first respect ourselves and give respect. Life provides us a two-way street, and while some travel down a one-way path to get to their destination, I find that it is best to exhibit that which I desire. As the Golden Rule states: "Do Unto Others As You Would Have Them Do Unto You." Get the love and respect you deserve by being the love and respect you want.

We are all mirrors, so let us reflect light, love, and truth!

THE PRECIOUS GEM COLLECTION

SELF-ACCEPTANCE

You are the one person that you will be bound to your whole life, so you might as well accept yourself as the wonderful, uniquely designed individual you are. If you don't accept yourself for who you are, imperfections and faults included, then you will find it that much harder to accept the faults and imperfections in others. We are whole and complete individuals, and like anything else in life, we all possess an opposite. We often hear that there are two sides to every story, two sides to every coin, the yin and yang, hot and cold, big and small, up and down, light and dark, love and hate, and so forth and so on. We need opposites so that we remain balanced in such a complex world, one filled with tons of intricacies. We can't know one without the other. We all have our sweet and sour points, but we must accept the whole of who we are, not just in part. The beauty of it all is the fact that we all share common ground with every human being walking the earth. Yes, we all may be different in so many ways, right on down to our fingerprints and DNA, but we all share faults and imperfections that come in different shapes and sizes. However, at the very core of our existence lies a root of imperfection that is familiar to everyone. Additionally, it is when you can find beauty in every imperfection that makes room for a bit of perfection.

CHAPTER 4

***

TRANSCEND

Emerge. Evolve. Transform. Transcend.

THE PRECIOUS GEM COLLECTION

WHAT MOVES YOU?

What gets you out of bed every morning? What drives you? Where does your passion reside? Do you let love rule in your heart, or does fear take precedence? What moves you?

Some say that fear is one of the greatest motivators, but it is also one of the greatest dream killers. If fear is moving you to do whatever you do on a regular basis, then you must ask yourself a question: "What will I do when the fear is gone?" Most people spend their whole life living in fear; fear of failure and fear of success are two of the major components. All the while, they should be asking themselves what fear really is.

Fear is an illusion. Fear seeks to keep you in a rut. Fear is a silent killer that slowly deteriorates your dreams. Fear promotes procrastination, stagnation, and agitation. Fear holds you hostage and cripples you, leaving you with little to no hope of forward progression. Fear creeps around in your mind just waiting to attack. It gives you all the reasons why anything you choose to pursue won't work, and forces you to give up without even trying. Fear is your greatest enemy. Fear will create a futile existence for you and those close to you if you allow it. If you do not learn how to master and overcome your fears, you will become a slave to them, only doing what they move you to do. You will become restricted by its power over you, and the hold it has on you will eventually suffocate you. You will be bound by dissatisfaction, lifeless and afraid. In order to achieve greatness and fulfill your most sought after dreams Gems, you must first conquer your fears by doing exactly what you are afraid of doing (in moderation and safety of course)

So I ask you Gems…What moves you?

THE PRECIOUS GEM COLLECTION

BURDENS

Lay your burdens down and find rest. In God there is rest for the weary soul. You don't have to carry your burdensome load, for His yoke is easy and His burden is light Gems. Cast all of your cares on the Lord, for He cares for you. Don't you dare worry or become anxious, don't you know that God is in control and has already made a way? Trust Him, you'll see! Just rest…

"Casting all your care upon him; for he careth for you…But the God of all grace, who hath called us unto his eternal glory by Christ Jesus, after that ye have suffered a while, make you perfect, establish, strengthen, settle you. To him be glory and dominion for ever and ever. Amen." (1 Peter 5:7-KJV)

THE PRECIOUS GEM COLLECTION

I AM FOUND

Life is one of the greatest gifts God has given to each of us. Life is an opportunity for us to unveil every spectacular part of who we are. If we don't take the time to find out who we truly are, we fail to unlock our beautiful essence, and then we become susceptible to society's definition of who we *ought* to be. If we don't look deep within ourselves, in the very pockets of our hearts and souls where the hidden treasure of our being lies, we will fall prey to the opinions of others. We will become lost in someone else's reality, lost in the pages of our lives that were left undone, the pages that were never filled because we were afraid to unlock the door to self. When we look for pieces of ourselves in others, trying to fit into a puzzle that was not designed for us, we fail to realize that there is a beautiful life within waiting to unfold. We do more of an injustice to ourselves when living vicariously through someone else. While the person we are living through is living their life, the life we so desperately want to live, the life we think we want to live, we neglect our own precious life, allowing it to slip away into the hands of the unknown. Therefore, this then leaves us stuck being a mere copy of something that was not intended for us to mimic, while our original self is locked away deep down inside.

Ask yourself today Gems, do you want to be a mere copy, or do you want to be a unique and divinely designed original? We each have a mind, body and soul uniquely designed and tailored to fit our very own personality and purpose. There is a purpose designated for every, single one of us. It is up to us to search within the depths of our soul to find it. I'll give you a little hint, it tends to roam around in your heart just waiting for you to notice it, nurture it, and walk in it. You hold the key to the knowledge of self, unlock the door! The answers to the questions you hold deep inside are within your reach, grab ahold of it! You hold the map to the hidden treasures of your heart, find it! The visions that are dear to you are yours for a reason. Hold them close to your heart and don't let them go. All that you are, God has already placed on the inside of you. Look within!

Emerge. Evolve. Transform. Transcend.

THE PRECIOUS GEM COLLECTION

Affirmation: I AM A CHILD OF GOD, WISE, GUIDED, AND LOVED.

Be the best you that you can be Precious Gems, live your best life to the fullest!

Emerge. Evolve. Transform. Transcend.

THE PRECIOUS GEM COLLECTION

A NEW DAY

It's a New Day! Let this be the day that you begin again. Start fresh and begin anew Gems. A new chapter of your life is at hand and life is waiting for you to turn the page. A clean slate awaits you and an empty canvas waiting to be filled. Live, love, forgive and give. Let go of the past and put yesterday away. Live for the moment and enjoy today. Don't fret upon tomorrow, tomorrow will worry about itself. Plan, prepare and pray for the road that lies ahead of you. Stay focused. Dream. Hope. Inspire. Achieve. Don't you dare give up! You are that much closer to fulfilling your destiny. There's a lot more life for you to live. While no one knows what tomorrow will bring, you do have the right to hope for the best. Breathe easy today and release all stress. No more tears upon your pillow. No more room for sorrow. You're being cleansed, purified and healed. Free yourself. Let your soul fly. Life is beautiful. Life is a gift. Love is all there is. You are not alone Gems. The universe conspires to bless you today, and every single day that follows. With an open heart and arms wide open you are received, you are accepted and you are loved. You are held in the highest regard. Positive energy surrounds you.

The world is your stage Precious Gems, light it up!

THE PRECIOUS GEM COLLECTION

ASSURANCE

What I realize now more than ever Gems, is that God has had His hand on me way before I even reached my hand out to Him. As I look back over my life and take inventory, all I can say is "Thank you Jesus." Thank you for the times when a way was made out of no way. Thank you for being my guiding light and bringing me back every time I lost my way. Thank you for the many blessings, and unmerited favor during times when only a miracle would suffice. Thank you for the many angels, friends, family members and strangers that have come into my life at the perfect, anointed and appointed time. Thank you for being my strength when I was weak. Thank you for allowing me to be humble and meek, even in the face of adversity. Thank you for the constant reassurance that the victory is mine indeed. Thank you for the peaks, hills and the valleys that gave me the strength and enabled me to walk in the fullness of who I was created to be.

You see Gems, there have been many times when sorrow heavily outweighed my joy. However, it was during those times when I saw myself clearer than ever before. You see Gems, while anguish and pain try to tear you down, it truly seeks to make you stronger and prepare you for the best that is yet to come. Don't you know that you were born to win, and that all things work together for good? You are victorious! With all that said, I encourage you to take a look at yourself and claim the victory over your life. Look back only long enough to see just how far you've come, and look ahead towards the bright future that awaits you. We are all human and imperfect by nature. However, the beauty about life is that we are not called to be perfect. We are called to be who we were created to be, and to walk in the fullness of it. We must improve upon our imperfections as best we can. Take steps forward, and leave the rest in God's capable and willing hands. We all have a place to be on this earth, and a seat to fill. Look deep within yourself to find out just where you belong Gems, I guarantee you it's a very special place!

THE PRECIOUS GEM COLLECTION

DEFINE WHO YOU ARE

Define who you are or someone else may define you for you. Too often individuals allow others to dictate their reality and define who they are for them. We are all unique, special, and distinct beings. We all have a place on this earth, a role to play, and a seat to fill. We all possess a spirit within that enables us to be, and do what we were called to do. People try to intimidate, discourage, belittle, ostracize, overpower and oppress others in order to get ahead in life. However, that is the cowardly way to go about things, because no one person is worth more than another. We were all created to be equal, and we were all born and have been granted the same right to life. Instead of stepping on one another to get to the top, one should be encouraging, uplifting, inspiring, motivating, supporting, and nudging one another in the right direction on this journey. Everyone wants to be the top dog over the underdog, but when we come to the realization that we are all in the same game, running in the same race, and trying to make it across the finish line, only then will we be able to truly soar to higher heights and achieve greatness. Don't allow anyone to tell you that you *cannot* accomplish what you endeavor to achieve, because you *can* do all things through Christ which strengthens you. Do not allow anyone to tell you that you *are not* good enough, because you *are* good enough. Do not allow anyone to tell you that there *isn't* room for you in this race, because we *each* have our very own lane. Stand for something Gems, because if you stand for nothing, you will fall for everything.

KNOW WHO YOU ARE!
KNOW WHOSE YOU ARE!
NEVER FORGET WHERE YOU CAME FROM!
KNOW WHERE YOU ARE GOING!

Walk in your purpose Gems. The world is yours, and it is right at your fingertips. You hold the paintbrush and the paint, and each day is like a blank canvas ready to be filled. It's time to paint a new picture on the canvas of life.

Emerge. Evolve. Transform. Transcend.

THE PRECIOUS GEM COLLECTION

CHOICES

Misery loves company, but that does not mean that one should join forces with misery in order to accommodate sorrow. Happiness sometimes stands alone, but one should never compromise their joy in order to grant misery's wish.

We live in a world where hope is fleeting, and it is often difficult for one to live free and unencumbered. Many walk around carrying the weight of the world on their shoulders, often burdened by the pangs of life. We live in a cold world, and it is a harsh reality. However, one does not have to be chilled by the terms of an inclement society. Hold on to your joy, for there resides your strength. Do your best not to gravitate towards misery or grant it the power it does not deserve. We all have to cry sometimes. We all fall down sometimes, and we all face adversity. However, we do not have to live in a pit of sorrow that does not enable us to grow. We have to fight to stay up. We have to live in order to learn. We have to fall in order to rise sometimes.

Choose life today and love will follow. Choose peace today and let go of sorrow. Choose joy today and it will carry over into tomorrow. I know that life is not easy Gems. However, once you realize that your perspective in and/or about life will determine what the outcome of each day will be, you will begin do all that you can to make the necessary adjustments to your perspective and ultimately transform your life. It all begins with a single thought, a change of mind that can and will change your life!

Keep smiling Gems and keep shining. Do not let the rain cloud your vision for a brighter future Gems, take the lead and move forward with the poise, grace and elegance of a Precious Gem.

May your days be infused with all of the joy and wonder a day can bring. Let not your hearts be troubled by the things you have no control over Gems, but instead rejoice in the fact that you have lived to see another day.

THE PRECIOUS GEM COLLECTION

CHANGE OF HEART

You have the right to change your mind. Have you ever made a decision that felt right initially, but then it plagued you and did not sit well with you at all later on down the line? Did you force yourself to stick with the choice you made, while holding on to the belief that the commitment you made was etched in stone? Did your choice leave you feeling like there was absolutely no way out? Did you go against your true feelings and stay in a situation that jeopardized your total well-being? However, after all was said and done, did you later regret it? If you answered yes to any of these questions, you are officially human Gems!

We have all been there at one time or another, for there is no one perfect being walking the earth. Whether it is a career move, relationship, relocation, family decision, friendship, or simply not following one's intuition or gut feeling, we have all walked the path in one form or another. Sometimes we feel that every choice we make constitutes finality, and even though every decision carries its own set of weights, the reality is that we do have the right to change our minds. We must ultimately choose what is right for us, the best possible choice. Only you as an individual know what is right for you or what you will or will not tolerate. Only you can choose your highest form of good with the help and guidance of the Lord. People can counsel you and give you advice until they are blue in the face, but ultimately it is *you* who has to choose in the end.

You must also remember that to choose is to make a new way. In addition, *not* to choose is also a choice in and of itself. So Gems, on this day, choose what's best for you. You deserve nothing less than the best that is due to you. The blessing is that life will sometimes force you to move beyond your comfort zone, past your fears, pre-conceived notions, inhibitions and restrictions in order to fill the seat that life has reserved for you.

THE PRECIOUS GEM COLLECTION

IF THE GIFT IS STILL GOOD
IT IS NOT THE END!

People are often quick to cite that their days of utilizing a specific talent are over. They feel that time has ran out, or is running out. However, what one fails to realize is that it's never too late to pursue a dream, perfect a craft or live out a passion. If the gift is still good and the desire is still in your heart, then it is not the end. As a matter of fact Gems, it is just the beginning! The talent you possess is yours for a reason. We all have certain gifts that are unique to us as individuals, and we all have different desires. However, it is up to us to utilize and make the most of what we have been given, even as we evolve.

If is in your heart to sing, dance, entertain, write, cook, fly, teach, save lives, defend, mentor, serve, protect, start your own company, coach, or whatever else you may desire to do, it is up to you to do what fulfills you and makes you happy. It all begins with Self Gems, and *nobody* can tell *you* what makes *you* happy. Moreover, no one on earth can take your place or fill your seat. There is a special place for every single one of us on this earth, and it is *you* who has to take the necessary steps to fulfilling *your* destiny. The great thing about life Gems, is that the road tends to curve to accommodate us along the way. There is always help and support on the journey towards destiny. One must also remember that the greatest blessings are sometimes disguised as friends, strangers, colleagues, family members, life lessons and even missed opportunities. Have you ever wanted to pursue something and it just did not quite work out at a certain time, but when seasons changed another opportunity came along that was surprisingly better than the first? Well Gems, the key is to be ready for that opportunity when it comes, for when preparation meets opportunity, that's when the real magic happens. While all things take time to blossom, the key is to never give up, for in due season it will flourish. Go after your dreams Gems, and run the race that is set before you with endurance, patience and perseverance. The sky is the limit!

THE PRECIOUS GEM COLLECTION

FALL IN LOVE WITH YOUR LIFE

Fall in love with your life Gems, and challenge yourself to grow past your current reality. As human beings, we tend to focus so much on the past that we forget to be present in the moment. We lose our fervor for life as we try to hold on to the things of yesterday, and we get stuck in a rut that does not allow us to grow. We fight change, and we try so hard to stay in the comfort zone that once nurtured and protected us. However, all that does is hold us captive and leave us smothered by those very things that provided us with comfort for so long. We are afraid to climb higher or soar to heights unimaginable because we don't believe enough in our dreams. We spend most of our time doing what we *"have"* to do, and we sweep what we truly *want* to do under a rug, hoping that it will somehow bloom. If we allow life's challenges to stop us or stunt our growth, we will never dream or see beyond our current reality. We must not lose heart or our vision for the future, nor should we place so many limitations on the present and the power of God. While one must focus on reality in order to live, we must not forget that without a fresh vision we are prone to perish.

Believe again, fall in love with your life and turn your dreams into reality. Take hold of positive visualization and begin to imagine yourself exactly where you want to be. Start doing the things that your heart has spoken of for so long. Unlock the treasure of your soul and live free. Liberate yourself from all bondage. Break the chains that have you bound by fear and doubt. There is nothing in this world that you can't do. It all begins with one thought activated by faith, put into action by belief, and pursued with love. It's all inside Gems, you hold the key, and it is *you* who must first believe in all that *you* can be!

Trust and believe that someone is rooting for you, holding your hand, wishing upon a star for you, missing you, loving you, thinking of you, praying for you and holding you in consciousness each day.

THE PRECIOUS GEM COLLECTION

MANIFEST THE GREATNESS WITHIN

May these words resonate with your heart, mind and spirit as they speak life and shed light!

As a prelude to this inspiration, I want you all to bring into remembrance a moment in your life where you felt inadequate because everywhere you looked you saw no reflection of the beauty in your own soul. At that moment, were you nudged in the right direction or quickly reminded by another individual of the greatness you possessed within? While many of us can answer this question positively, let us remember today all those who cannot. Many people roaming the earth lack the positive reinforcements and validation necessary to maintain a worthwhile existence. In addition, they may not even know where to begin. So, on this day, as we go about our daily activities and follow through with our normal agendas, let us take the time to impact the life of another. Always remember that there is no gift too small. Smile at someone, it just may change their life. Be who you are and walk in the fullness of it, you just might enable someone to live out their own greatness. Don't let anyone sway your heart in a direction that is not true to your original self. And please, please don't let anyone steal your joy, take your pride or place limitations on you because of their own insecurity. Each of you represent greatness, so why wait to manifest it? The world is your stage Gems, go ahead and light it up!

My thoughts and prayers are with you Precious Gems, as well as my most sincere wishes. May your days be illuminated with the brightest light, and infused with all of the love, joy, and peace possible.

THE PRECIOUS GEM COLLECTION

WE'RE ALL IN NEED OF LOVE

For everyone out there struggling to make it through the day and hoping for a brighter existence, do not give up hope. While life on earth can sometimes breed a sense of futility, there is still hope for better days. All you have to do is wake up, get out of bed and trust that God gave you a life to behold this very day for reasons greater than what the naked eye can sometimes see. You have a purpose, and while it may not be clearly defined in a manual and handed to you at birth, trust and believe that each day reveals a piece to the puzzle. The journey is to be enjoyed, as life is a journey and not a destination. Yes, it gets real tough at times Gems, but I believe that anything worth having is worth fighting for. There is so much to pull from in this life, and all you have to do is just open your eyes to the good that surrounds you. Life is really beautiful Gems. I attribute the love I have in my heart to all of the love I have been given, and I want to pass it on. Gems, even if there is a time when you feel that love is absent, look inside yourself and grab a hold of the love that lives in you. I cannot express it enough in words just how powerful love is. Love has to be the greatest gift one could ever give or receive. While I may not have the opportunity to sit down and enjoy a conversation with each of you face to face, I am grateful for every chance that I get to communicate with you Precious Gems via inspiration. As I am granted breath of life each day, I pray that you all receive your heart's desire.

Gems, for every tear you have had to cry, love is on the way. For every time you were lied to or betrayed, love is on the way. For every time you went without a hand to hold, love is on the way. For every time someone broke your heart, love is on the way. For every time hope was lost, love is on the way. For every time your dreams were deferred, love is on the way. For every time love was absent, love is on the way.

Don't you dare give up hope, love is on the way!

THE PRECIOUS GEM COLLECTION

SHORT & SWEET

Run the race that is set before you with ENDURANCE, PATIENCE, and PERSEVERANCE. The race is not given to the swift, but to the one who can endure to the end.

People may try to break you down, steal your joy and take your pride, but they can't win. Be confident, steadfast, and unmovable. Believe in yourself. Have faith. Do not fear the unknown, you cannot lose. Bring your A-game and put your best foot forward. Give life the best you've got! In addition, if you should lose your way or come up short, always remember that nothing in life is ever really lost. Even when you think you have failed miserably, take a closer look and see that you have actually gained something more, something priceless. You won a new experience, gained increased knowledge, learned another lesson, gained strength, courage, and most of all wisdom. Look to the future. Let go of the past. Live in the present, and live it to the fullest. You are more than conquerors Gems!

THE PRECIOUS GEM COLLECTION

INTUITION

There is a little voice on the inside of you that speaks softly, and gently nudges you in the right direction. However, this is the little voice that we tend to ignore, block out and dismiss. It is called an intuitive sense, the act of knowing or sensing without rationalization. We all have intuition, and sometimes we may not even know why our spirit may be telling us one thing, when we are presented with another. In our dealings with human beings, we tend to go by what we hear and see. We tend to cling to those things which are tangible, rather than to the things we know instinctually. Has there ever been a time in your life when someone said something to you, and even though it sounded good, your spirit still said something is not right, it does not add up? Has there ever been an incidence when someone or something may have appeared bad to you, but your spirit told you otherwise and spoke of its goodness? That is when our intuitive sense comes into play, and we must use discernment in order to decipher the messages that God sends us. It is not always easy to be in tune with our spirit and that is why we must put it into practice. It is not a loud voice; it is a very gentle and soft voice. It is most often the loud voice of confusion, fear and doubt that drowns out the soft voice and causes us not to be in tune with the spirit within. We must learn to trust our instincts, and we must pay attention to that little nudging on the inside of us that informs us when something is either right or wrong. There have been many times in my life when my spirit nudged me to do something, take heed or simply acquiesce in a place of peace in order to take hold of revelation. Instead of me acting promptly and obeying my spirit, I began to rationalize and talk myself out of things. In the end, this only led to me delaying a process that God had already set in motion, while causing my spirit to be disrupted. Have you ever felt something in your gut and it just felt right? You may not have been able to pin point it or even have a good understanding of what you were feeling, but all you knew was that you felt it deep down in your soul.

THE PRECIOUS GEM COLLECTION

It may not make sense at all in the natural, but supernaturally it makes perfect sense. God works in mysterious ways and it will most often seem peculiar, but He knows exactly what He is doing. Pay attention to those little nudges that tug at your heart strings, there's a lesson and a blessing attached!

THE PRECIOUS GEM COLLECTION

SERENDIPITY

An amazing thing happened to me the other day. I ran into an old friend and had one of the best conversations of my life. It was almost like I was sitting in front of a mirror, staring into love, wisdom, experience, strength, growth, contentment, and sincerity. I must be honest, there are often times when my current schedule does not even permit me to sit down and really breathe the way I should, let alone have a long, drawn out, deep, heartfelt conversation. However, on this particular day, I decided to simply breathe and sit still long enough to actually listen to what my own heart was saying. You know what it said Gems? It said, "it's okay Ajá, you can take a break from life today."

As the world turns, there will always be things to tend to, errands to run, phone calls to make, bills to pay, people to see, and tons of work to do in general. However, it is in those priceless moments of solitude or in the company of someone special when you are truly able to let go and see a reflection of yourself, or perhaps a glimpse of what you would like to avail yourself to more often, such as simple abundance! Sometimes the simplest things in life are the most prolific, and most often the most prevalent. The best things in life are free. The most priceless gift someone can give you is love straight from their heart. Take the time to enjoy the company of another human being and you just might see a reflection of the same charisma, joy, love, peace and beautiful soul you possess.

We cross paths with tons of people each day, never really taking the time to look deeper than the surface. However, when we do take a closer look, we give two worlds a chance to collide and forever change in the most profound and amazing way!

THE PRECIOUS GEM COLLECTION

MISCOMMUNICATION

Have you ever said something to someone, only to find out later that the message behind the statement expressed was misconstrued? Was the intent behind the words spoken misunderstood, leading you to reexamine what you said, while trying to fit yourself into the mode you were in at the time, along with the tone you held and the state of mind you were in when you first said it?

For this very reason, it is pertinent that we are clear and concise in our dealings with others. As human beings we have a way with words, and while some things are universal, we must remember that some things are not. Different cultures view things differently. While we live in a huge world where it is easily assumed that everyone speaks the same language, we must remember that everyone does not. Some cultures hold tightly to certain things. Language is held sacred in a lot of cultures, and words can hold a negative or positive connotation depending on the way it is used. I guarantee you that if we all took a trip around the world we would all see in plain view exactly what I am conveying through this message. The beauty of it all Gems, is that this kaleidoscope of lifestyles, values, cultures, beliefs, and languages grants us a priceless picture of the world. It enables us to appreciate and enjoy our very own culture, while experiencing and learning about the cultures of others.

We must be careful what we say and how we say it. We live in a world where things are easily taken out of context, misunderstood and often twisted. It's nobody's fault particularly, it's just the way of the world. However, we must try our very best to ensure that the messages we send do come across the right way. It is up to us to begin with clarity to ensure that we are met at the best level of comprehension. We do not want to offend someone because we lack awareness in a certain area, instead we should make an effort to be as aware as we possibly can. The world is a beautiful and spectacular place. Let's enjoy our world and make the best of every encounter Gems!

THE PRECIOUS GEM COLLECTION

BUTTERFLIES

Sometimes people alight upon our lives like butterflies in the spring and they light up our souls. They start a party in our hearts, leaving us with a feeling of inexplicable joy that runs over into our future. It's almost like they are angels acting as strangers and friends. And, without any explanation, they do our hearts a world of good. They enter our lives at a certain time, and whether it is for a single precious moment, a specific reason, a season or a lifetime, they always seem to leave footprints in our hearts. They gently guide us along our way. They hold our hands through the storms of life, and simply brighten up our days here on earth. They completely and utterly change our lives! They serve as special little reminders that God still has our back and is watching over us daily, reassuring us that everything will be okay.

We have all encountered a special being at one time or another, and if we look back on our lives, we will notice that it was always at the perfect time, a time when we needed it most. Do you remember your very first encounter with a beautiful butterfly? I am sure that it took your mind off of everything else that may have been clouding your thoughts. Take the time to smile, it's contagious. Take the time to sing, it activates joy. Take the time to believe, it just might give you wings. Take the time to stop and smell the roses, it's a fragrance you'll never want to forget. Most importantly Gems, take the time to love, it never runs out.

THE PRECIOUS GEM COLLECTION

CHAPTER 5

***

SOAR

THE PRECIOUS GEM COLLECTION

SPREAD YOUR WINGS AND FLY...

May this message greet you with love, and leave you in an inexplicable state of peace that transcends all understanding on today. The meaning of this message is so very close to my heart. For those of you who know me, you know that I am absolutely enamored by and in love with butterflies. However, for those of you who do not know this about me, I will give you a brief introduction.

You see, while nature is filled with so many beautiful creatures and unique entities, I have found butterflies to really represent something special. If you look closely at yourself and life, you may even be able to compare yourself to something in nature that perhaps reflects a part of your character or personality. Butterflies represent transformation and growth in my life. They are free-spirited and boundless, beautiful and delicate, as they emerge from the very cocoon that serves to protect and nurture them until they are ready to soar. As I look back at my every encounter with a beautiful monarch or tiger swallowtail, I begin to see a pattern in my own life.

You see Gems, there was a time when butterflies may have been overlooked by me because my focus was so obscured by the "major" things going on around me. One might ask how one could neglect to see the beauty that surrounds them in nature. Well Gems, the answer might be the same for a multitude of people. It is so easy to get caught up in a daily routine, focusing more on the destination rather than the journey. However, life certainly has a way of grabbing your attention, and for me it took a bittersweet awakening to open my eyes to the things I had been overlooking around me. My life-changing experience occurred on June 18th, 2001, my 20th birthday. My Grandmother Ida Vera passed away on that day, and her death changed my life profoundly through the shaping of my character. She was my angel walking the earth, a sheer inspiration. When something so unexpected occurs in one's life, you begin to change the way you see life to a certain extent.

Emerge. Evolve. Transform. Transcend.

THE PRECIOUS GEM COLLECTION

It's almost like you begin to live every single moment to the fullest, taking a picture in your mind of every special memory, and letting go of anything that weighs you down. For me her death brought on a sort of rebirth, as I emerged from a cocoon that kept me sheltered all of my life. I began to spread my wings and fly, while letting go of fear and all of the things that tried so hard to keep me from dreaming, seeking and reaching for higher. I really saw a change in myself. I was no longer afraid to breathe, explore, or follow my heart.

Life is a gift Gems, and each day we are granted an opportunity to unravel it piece by piece. It's almost like the sun is a beautiful gold ribbon carefully wrapped around the package of life that was specially designed for each of us, and all we have to do is unwrap it upon arising each day. Live your life today Gems. Seek and you will find what you are looking for. Reach for the sky, it will take you higher than you could possibly imagine. Spread your wings, you'll never know just how far you can fly until you try. Dream that dream that is deemed impossible, while believing that anything is possible. Keep moving forward on your journey through life, and only look back long enough to see just how far you have come. Don't dwell on the past, look towards the future. Speak life, for there is power in the spoken word. Surround yourself with positive energy, and make room for the best that is yet to come.

You are empowered to prosper Precious Gems!

THE PRECIOUS GEM COLLECTION

STAY FLY...LIVE LIFE!

Beauty without an intrinsic form of contentment is like a beautiful antique vase imported from Italy without the essence of the most beautiful flower in nature to take the place of destitution. We live in a society that places so much emphasis on the outward appearance, rarely giving attention to the inner portion of our existence such as the heart, the soul and the mind. We are warped into thinking that in order to be fly, sexy, or complete, we must wrap ourselves in the latest, most sought after gear on the market, and we lose ourselves in the process. Now don't get me wrong Gems, I myself am a shoe and handbag fan. I love the shoes Gems! However, I have learned that a sexy pair of shoes and a sharp bag doesn't go very far without a beautiful heart. What lies within is what makes us shine, and if that's not the case, then we are allowing the clothes, shoes, bags and hats to make us. We then begin to take on the personality of a material object, rather than allowing our own essence to shine forth. Have you ever seen a lady or gentleman walking down the street in a sharp outfit and said to yourself, "Wow, they are really working that outfit?" Have you ever also gone home and looked into your own closet to find something that would enhance your very own style? We all do it, but do we ever really stop and say: "Wow! That person has a beautiful smile, or that person has an aura that just lights up the room?" Is it really stressed in our society to look beyond the surface? Quite frankly, the answer is no. I say this to say that while it is important to keep up our appearance and remain well groomed, it is also equally important to maintain our mental, emotional and spiritual well-being. Do you know how fly you are Gems, regardless of age, gender, height, weight, size or shape? You are spectacular Gems! I just want you all to be able to flaunt that beautiful inner spirit, that heart of gold, that sexy smile, that aura of light, that soul refined, that renewed mind and all of the wonderful things that each and every one of you possess. You are who you are Gems, and *you* are enough! Take the time to look into your own heart and allow yourself to see the beauty that you possess.

Emerge. Evolve. Transform. Transcend.

THE PRECIOUS GEM COLLECTION

Don't be afraid to let your light shine, you illuminate this life upon every step you take. Hold your head up high! You are beautiful in mind, body and soul, so let is shine as you continue to grow.

THE PRECIOUS GEM COLLECTION

WHAT IS YOUR MISSION STATEMENT?

A dear friend recently asked me why I wrote, and while the answer did come quite easily, the question did cause me to reflect. As I look back over my life, I have found that writing has not only been cathartic for me, but also a way for me to teach, inspire, and uplift. When I was a child I kept journals and diaries. Writing provided me with an open door, a way to express myself. As I made my transition from childhood into adulthood, writing not only served as a catalyst, but also as a form of enlightenment.

As my heart guides the pen, I dictate and the paper listens. There is nothing that I say that the paper can't handle. The paper is strong, receptive and resilient. Everything that flows from the waterfalls of my heart I jot down, and the paper complies. The paper allows free reign and unlimited opportunity. The paper holds no inhibitions, biased opinions or prejudices. The paper seeks to develop me as I aspire to learn, grow, achieve, teach and inspire. Never does it seek to put me down, hold me back, oppress me or put a dimmer on my light. While it holds transforming power, it never seeks to change me. The paper welcomes me with open arms, and no matter how many mistakes I make, or how many times I have to begin again, the paper is forgiving. It stands ready, always willing to grant me another chance. I can be exactly who I am, exactly who I want and need to be, nothing more, and nothing less. I can say what I want to say, the way I want to say it. The paper brings my thoughts to life, as my words tell a story of the past, present and future. It has become my playground, my empty canvas. I am free to paint whatever picture I want. I am the artist, my words are the paint. Every creation is the picture that lives in my heart and flows as inspiration.

Precious Gems, whatever your mission statement is in life, be sure to carry it out with all of your heart, all of your mind, and all of your soul. Live out your passion, step on the scene and

THE PRECIOUS GEM COLLECTION

introduce yourself to the world. Be all of the YOU that you can be. You are who you are, and that's the gift!

The canvas awaits you, paint from the heart Precious Gems.

THE PRECIOUS GEM COLLECTION

CANVAS OF LIFE

Life is a beautiful gift to behold. Each new day grants you something new and wonderful, something splendid to look forward to. With each new day comes a chance to paint a new picture on the canvas of life with a fresh coat of passion, inspiration and a vivid vision. The dawn of a new day erases the agenda of the past, and it illuminates the present with hope for a brighter future.

Take hold of today Gems and create a whole new world. Make use of what's available to you, while upholding gratitude and grace. The world is your playground, chase after your dreams. Seek and you will find what you are looking for. Dreams do come true. Cultivate your talents and cherish your current reality, for every precious moment is a gift.

Don't you dare look at the negative and make it your foundation, instead make it a stepping stone and climb higher. Grab a hold to the positive and make that your foundation. Surround yourself with all that's good, and even when you find yourself surrounded by the dark shadows of the world, look ahead, illumination awaits you. Paint a new picture Gems, the canvas awaits you!

THE PRECIOUS GEM COLLECTION

WINDOW TO YOUR SOUL

Have you ever looked into the eyes of another human being and saw the beauty inside of their soul? Did it strike a chord with you and render you speechless for more than what seemed to be an eternity? Did you catch a glimpse of the genuine and sincere qualities that are very much necessary in the world today?

Well Gems, I had an encounter of this sort today, and it touched me in a way that words cannot explain. So often we neglect to see beyond the surface of an individual, holding their name and face up to a certain standard. We fail to realize that there is a heart that beats inside of that individual, a soul that feels and yearns to be fed, a mind that can encompass more than one can imagine, a past filled with memories of both joy and pain, an awareness that is refreshing, and a consciousness that seeks to enlighten everyone who enters their path. When one possesses a vision that enables and encourages those who seek knowledge and wisdom to easily attain it, one can't help but to be inspired. It is in those rare and precious moments when you are captivated by the soul of another, a moment where only tears of joy and gratitude will suffice. Sometimes words get in the way, and perhaps it is true what they say about the eyes being the window to the soul. For this very reason, I count every encounter with a kindred spirit as a priceless gift.

I share this verse with you, as it has been true for me on many occasions. I want to dedicate this message to all of the individuals who have touched my life, made me laugh, brightened up my day, left footprints in my heart and who have been my angels along the way. Thank you for shining your light in my life Precious Gems, and for allowing me to share my journey of inspiration with you.

"Be careful to entertain strangers, for you never know when you may have unwittingly entertained an angel." ~ Hebrews 13:2 (NIV)
May your day be infused with love, peace, joy, and beauty within your soul!

THE PRECIOUS GEM COLLECTION

THE GIFT OF SOLITUDE

Sometimes the greatest gift one can give of oneself is sheer solitude. We spend most of our days and nights running around, often catering to the needs of others. We miss out on countless opportunities to abide in the bliss of solace, as we give our time and energy away freely to the events of the day. We wait until there is a dire need for solitude, either to escape the chaos of the day or some noisome ambiance. However, once one realizes that solitude is as much a necessity as it is a luxury, it will no longer be seen solely as a gift, but it will become a vital part of their daily existence.

It is so very necessary to take time out for yourself Gems, to give your mind, body and soul a rest. I spent some time in a café today with the company of myself, and it did wonders for my heart and soul. I almost forgot how good it felt to simply be with my own thoughts, my very own heartbeat, inhaling and taking in life, while looking out into the windows of the world. I almost forgot what it was like to admire people from all walks of life as they come and go as they please. They go about their daily routines while taking care of business, embarking on a journey towards their next destination upon every step. The hustle and bustle of NYC streets provides enough excitement for an entire day. The vendors, the shops, and the scent of the city alone are enough to make you smile, as there are a variety of sights to see.

Now Gems, spending time in solitude does not have to be a chore, it is supposed to be enjoyable. The start of a new day brings forth a kaleidoscope of alternatives, and once you avail yourself to solitude, you are granted an opportunity to engage in things that suit *your* tastes. There is always the cinema, a place where you can escape into fantasy land for an hour or two, as you delve into the lives of fictional/non-fictional characters. As the lives of others are being portrayed on the big screen, your own imagination begins to soar. There is always a walk in the park, for nature is always soothing as it nourishes the soul. There are also museums, malls, bookstores, coffee shops and a plethora of other things awaiting your arrival.

THE PRECIOUS GEM COLLECTION

What I have learned in life Gems, is that sometimes the hardest thing for someone to do is spend time alone. However, if you just take a look at the beautiful, living spirit inside of you that others enjoy, imagine how much fun spending a day with yourself can be. Most often the clarity you seek is right within your reach, but it is often clouded by outside interference. Most often the answers you need are right in front of your face, but sometimes your vision is blurred by your surroundings. All that you need is available to you; all you have to do is just take the time to receive it. The more you acquiesce in a place of peace, the more peace will be bestowed upon you.

Enjoy life Gems! Enjoy your own company, and always remember that you are simply precious!

THE PRECIOUS GEM COLLECTION

PAIN IS A GIFT

Pain is the gift that nobody wants, but yet it still comes. Pain moves you. In life, we will be faced with trials and tribulation. However, the beautiful thing about the pain that challenges may bring, is the fact that we come out much stronger, wiser and that much more courageous. In order to know joy, we must endure pain. In order to appreciate the sun, we must endure the rain. Life will sometimes deal you a hand that may seem difficult to play, but we all possess the potential to win and the power to choose. We can choose happiness over stress. We can choose peace over anxiety. We can choose freedom over bondage. Most importantly, we can choose love. It may not always be easy to see life through rose colored glasses or even see the glass as half full. However, if we just trust and believe that sunshine will break through the clouds and we hold onto hope, things will eventually start to look and feel a little better. Sometimes we may find ways to justify our pain in order to keep from breaking down, but the truth is Gems, pain is pain, and we all must experience it. We can either run from it, or we can stand and fight our way through it, knowing that the victory is ours. Always remember that seasons change, and so do we. The transforming power of pain prepares us for all of the joy that is due to each and every one of us once the storm passes. Even greater than that Gems, is the awesome power of prayer which heals and restores. Love is the ultimate power and thriving force. It will take you higher and be your anchor throughout raging storms. Love bears all things. Love believes all things. Love hopes all things. Love endures all things. Love never fails. So, continue making room for love and let love reign!

THE PRECIOUS GEM COLLECTION

ONE WISH

If I had one wish, there would always be sunshine to brighten up your lives. If I had one wish, it would be to share all the love I have with those who never even had a smidgen of love to give. If I had one wish, it would be to take away the tears of the earth and replace it with all my joy. If I had one wish, it would be to erase all of the pain and provide a serene escape for those in need. If I had one wish, there would be unity and no separation. If I had one wish, there would be no lies or pain from deceit. If I had one wish, there would be less crime and more peace. If I had one wish, every storm that passed over our lives would be one that only came to cleanse, heal and restore. If I had one wish Gems, love would be the constant and thriving force of the universe, and good would always win. Kindness would overrule the harsh ways of the world forever.

For every person who receives this message, there will be many who benefit from the meaning behind it. Don't you know that every single time you are touched in a positive way you then somehow pass it on to someone else? In addition, they then do the same, either consciously or subconsciously, as they pass the baton in their own special way to someone else. It then becomes a sort of kindness crusade that started with a single touch from someone's heart, causing a domino effect of kindness that all started with a single act.

Gems, I think my wish is somehow coming true!

THE PRECIOUS GEM COLLECTION

TEN HUT!

Just as gold must pass through the fire in order to be refined, just as an oyster must endure pain and discomfort in order to produce a beautiful pearl, and just as coal must be put under pressure in order for a beautiful diamond to be formed, we as human beings must sometimes endure hardship in order to be purified.

You see Gems, there may be times when you feel that struggle is your plight day in and day out. However, while pain we may sometimes eat for breakfast, lunch, and dinner, let us not forget that strength is our dessert. If going through the fire means coming out as gold, then so be it! There will be mountains to climb, valleys that bring us down, pits that seem too deep, storms that may last too long, challenges to overcome, hurdles to jump over, battles to fight, lessons to learn and tests to endure. However, with all of the things that may try to break you down, they are in essence in place to build you up Gems. Each one of us, at one time or another has had to put on mental, emotional and spiritual armor in order to trek through life's rough terrain and face raging battles. But you see Gems, the battle is not yours, it's the Lord's! And, even in your weakness His power is made strong. So keep up the good fight of faith and put on the full armor of God.

You are in it to win it Gems, and you are more than conquerors! Endure hardness as good soldiers and endure to the end. The victory is already yours.

THE PRECIOUS GEM COLLECTION

DYNAMITE

How can I elevate my humanity? How do I transcend myself and utilize my purpose for a greater good? How do I remain in alignment with the Creator of the universe in order to elevate my soul to higher heights?

As I read these words aloud, and once over in my head, I cannot not help but to meditate on them for a moment. These questions hold such power, and while the answers may not come speedily, it does reside in a place within each of our souls, ready and willing to rise to the surface at the appropriate time. As one seeks to answer questions of this sort, the realization of self and the duty of self will certainly become quite evident. Furthermore, for one to even ask these questions means that one's soul has been elevated to a level that is no longer selfish, but rather selfless.

You see Gems, walking in the fullness of who you were created to be not only benefits you as an individual, but it also affects the world at large. Once you begin to fully accept, embrace and love who you are as a whole and complete individual, you will then be able to perform selfless acts that not only contribute to humankind as a whole, but also affect change and transform the dynamic of society. Your inquisitive nature will be heightened. Your intuitive sense will serve a greater purpose as you begin to trust your instincts more and more. Your awareness will be raised as you hold in consciousness the entities that would ordinarily be overlooked. As you delve into your own heart and the hearts of others, you will then begin to see that the common denominator is love. Everyone needs love, and right along with food, clothing and shelter, it is a necessity!

We live in a cold world, and it is a harsh reality. It is so easy to become complacent in a world that seeks to leave us tainted with disappointment, confusion, fear and darkness. However, we must not succumb. Don't let the pangs of this life stain your existence with negativity. Instead, transcend the dire ways of the world by loving, living and laughing in the face of every evil. We still hold the right to acquiesce in a place of peace and love that totally

THE PRECIOUS GEM COLLECTION

transcends the ills of the world.

We each possess an inherent power and will to survive. We are natural born fighters in the sense that all we need is already deposited directly on the inside of us, such as strength, courage and wisdom. It's almost like a stick of dynamite. When you look at dynamite, it does not particularly appear to be something that could blow things to smithereens. However, if you take a look inside and simply light the fire, all will be set ablaze in a matter of seconds. It's not what's on the outside that did the job. It's what lies at the center, at the core of your very being that causes the huge blast. So often we look outside of ourselves for the answers that live within. Look within Gems, it's all inside.

THE PRECIOUS GEM COLLECTION

ENLARGE YOUR VISION

A new year is upon us Gems, and we must be careful to look beyond our immediate circumstances and into a brighter future. Forgetting what is behind, we must move forward, and press on towards the great things ahead of us.

So often we as human beings get so caught up on what is right within our grasp, forgetting to hope, dream and envision a better and brighter future. However, we must keep on expecting, believing, and declaring God's best over our lives. Once you begin to see things on a greater scale and through a wider scope, then and only then will you be able to see a positive change. Sometimes we dream the "possible" dream, when we should be dreaming the "impossible" dream. I say impossible to challenge you to think and dream beyond what you believe is humanly attainable and get out of the *"safe-zone"* if you will, because once you realize that nothing is impossible, you will then be able to go after those dreams that may have been deemed unattainable.

Life affords us unlimited possibilities, unlimited growth, unlimited learning and unlimited opportunities. However, the limitations that we place on ourselves, and allow others to place on us, keep us from achieving, attaining, fulfilling, completing and succeeding at our dreams. Don't you know that we are boundless Gems? There is nothing on this earth that we can't do if we put our minds to it and trust in the Lord. Have you ever heard of positive visualization? It is a tactic often used to get one to visualize themselves in a situation of their desire. You imagine yourself doing or being exactly what you have dreamed about. It causes you to focus on what you really want as you enlarge your vision. You see, once you enlarge your vision, you then will be able to enlarge your territory. Territory meaning all of those things that you quickly dismiss in your mind, while your heart is still holding on to them. Sometimes we don't get what we desire because we don't believe we can obtain it. Sometimes we don't get that promotion because we don't believe we are qualified. Sometimes we don't get that new car or house because we don't believe we could ever afford it.

THE PRECIOUS GEM COLLECTION

Sometimes we don't receive that mate because we don't believe we deserve them. Sometimes we don't win that contest because we don't believe we ever had a chance of winning. Sometimes we miss out on our greatest blessings because we are stuck in the "I can't" frame of mind, when we should be taking hold of the "I can" state of mind.

Start looking through the eyes of faith Gems, and begin to see yourself as that happy, healthy and whole individual. Start affirming yourself positively every, single day. No matter how bleak your situation may appear, there is always a way out of what appears to be no way. Think thoughts of victory and not defeat. Think on abundance, favor, hope, and all things good. Have faith Gems, and believe in your dreams.

THE PRECIOUS GEM COLLECTION

SCARS

Scars are lasting signs of damage that stay with us and remind us of an occurrence that brought us pain in the past. Scars don't always have to represent physical damage, they can also be a representation of emotional and psychological damage as well. Scars most often represent something negative, like someone or something that hurt us. They plague us, and every time we come across that scar we are taken down memory lane and automatically reminded of what we felt at that moment in time. We play that memory over in our heads, hoping that if we just relive it again and again, it will somehow magically disappear and erase the pain. However, you must realize that as long as you replay negativity over in your mind, negativity is exactly what will live on in you. You will then begin to breathe, breed and be negativity. Scars don't have to serve as negative and constant reminders of pain. They can also serve as reminders of healing and the people, places and things that we have overcome.

You see Gems, no matter what you have been through in this life, you have the power to break a cycle, change your state of mind and work towards a better future. Nothing has the power to dictate your present and future except you and God. However, it is you who gives your God given right to life and power away when you live in the past and drag it along with you into your present and future. You do not have to live in bondage and be bound by the painful memories of your past. We have all suffered the ills of this world and the pangs of life that try so hard to beset us. However, you have the power to be loosed from the pain and negativity if you just believe in yourself and allow yourself to be free. It is not easy Gems, for you may have had some devastating and traumatizing events occur in your life. You may want to be helped, but you just may not know where to begin. There may not be the right words to say to ease your pain, and you may not be understood because no one has walked a mile in your shoes. Well, that is when the power of love comes into play. You see, while we get so hung up on words, sometimes we just miss the point.

THE PRECIOUS GEM COLLECTION

Sometimes a hug, a smile or simply taking someone by the hand, looking them in the eyes and saying "I believe in you" or "I am praying for you" will do what words or rationale can't do. We live in a dark world, and while we all may wish that everyone had the luxury of living a life filled with love and happiness. The reality is that there are people walking around brokenhearted, contrite in spirit, abased, oppressed, depressed, hopeless, afraid and confused. It's so easy for one to walk through this life and turn a blind eye to the things going on around them, but it's even easier to stop and take a closer look.

Gems, you have all changed someone's life. Additionally, while many of you may not have to deal with a quarter of what others in the world have had to face or face on a daily basis, I just want to encourage you to take a closer look. You just may change someone's life today! Somebody is living because you gave them hope for a brighter tomorrow by simply saying "It'll be okay." Somebody will follow their dreams because you encouraged them to keep trying. Somebody will find love again because you showed them love. Somebody will pass this on simply because you took the time to listen to your heart.

Gems, if I never say anything again that remotely moves you in this life, may this message move you to do exactly what your heart has been moving you to do. Let go of those things that are weighing you down. Let go of the past and the negativity it may hold. Let go of your doubts, fears and inhibitions. Let go and Let God! You are loved Gems, and you are never alone on this road. Look to the hills for your help, God is a very present help in times of trouble. Reach out to someone in need. You are changing the world one act of kindness at a time!

THE PRECIOUS GEM COLLECTION

SACRIFICE

Sometimes we are forced to deal with situations that do not exactly fit into our idealistic view of perfection. Sometimes we are obliged to operate under circumstances that we wouldn't normally function well under in order to gain strength, courage and wisdom. Sometimes we are summoned to take on tasks that we wouldn't prefer to just so that character can be built within. Sometimes we may even have to deal with individuals that we wouldn't ordinarily choose to so that necessary experience can be obtained. Sometimes the difficult things required of us are in essence the greatest things that could happen for ourselves and others. It is the ultimate sacrifice!

Sacrifice gives us the strength to do the things we have to do when we don't believe we can. Sacrifice means giving even when we feel that we have nothing left to give. Sacrifice means giving of yourself to enhance the well-being of another even when your own well-being is at stake. Sacrifice means putting up with difficulties a lot longer, because while coming to a prompt resolution may bring momentary comfort to a situation, waiting on the best resolution may enhance discomfort. The ability to endure the discomfort that waiting on a proper resolution can bring requires a higher degree of effort and resolve on one's part, but it is well worth the sacrifice in the end. Sacrifice should no longer be seen as a means to an end, it should be the fire that keeps you moving along on this journey even when the journey seems long and hard. It should be the passion in your soul and the desire in your heart that keeps you striving for higher even when you can't see the light at the end of the tunnel.
Sacrifice does not always have to be a huge affair filled with dramatics. It can be quite simple, but yet so powerful.

Make your sacrifice today, it just might do your soul or the soul of another a whole world of good. It's the little things in life that matter the most, and as they add up to the bigger things, the impact is far greater than one could have ever imagined. You just never know how an intelligible act of kindness can change the world. Make the ultimate sacrifice today Precious Gems, be kind

THE PRECIOUS GEM COLLECTION

and keep the well-being of others in mind! The Best Is Yet To Come!

THE PRECIOUS GEM COLLECTION

REDEFINE WHO YOU ARE

The one thing that I love about life, is that it will never allow you to escape the ineluctable gift of change. Change is inevitable, it is bound to happen. There is nothing that you can say or do to rid your life of change. It is an inescapable factor that in essence moves one along to higher heights. A world without change is like a moment lived without fresh air. If you don't experience the benefits of oxygen on a daily basis, you are bound to live no more. It's the same with change. Change moves you in a certain direction. Change pulls you out of the old and into the new. Change gives you a new perspective. Change takes you out of your comfort zone. Change causes you to rethink, reflect, reevaluate and redefine who you are. Change is the gift that most people run from, but yet is must come. If you want the same results, keep doing the same things.

While change is unavoidable, it still assists us through life in more ways than a state of stagnancy would. Change can be uncomfortable at times, causing us to resist and pull back from it. Change forces you beyond your preconceived notions, and it often pushes you to release your inhibitions. You may even have to do some reprogramming when change occurs. Things will not stay the same in life, they change from day-to-day. However, the good part about it is that you often grow through each and every change that you face. So often we get set in our ways, refusing to change and let go of the things that stagnate us, and they most often leave us paralyzed in a time warp. We would not dare to think, speak or act differently due to the fact that we may have been operating in our own custom way for so long. What about trying new things or even living outside of the box that society has placed us in at times? "It's unthinkable!" says the non-dreamer. It is unheard of for someone who has lived most of their life one way, to then all of a sudden try and change it up. Well Gems, I am here to tell you that it is never too late to change or work on the things that you would like to improve upon and/or release.

THE PRECIOUS GEM COLLECTION

There's no time like the present time. Instead of us appreciating life's changes, we often depreciate the value of change by ignoring it or not accepting it. Once we realize that change is a friend and not a foe, then we will be able to accept the things that we cannot change, while doing our best to change the things that we can. It isn't always easy, but it is definitely worth a try. It does not matter how old or how young you are. It does not matter where you come from or where you are going. It does not matter if you have a GED or a Ph.D. It does not matter if you are short or tall. It does not matter what the situation is, change does not discriminate. Take hold of the gift and make the best out of the life you were granted. All you need is breath of life, a fresh vision and a little faith. The rest will surely come!

THE PRECIOUS GEM COLLECTION

HAPPINESS

Sometimes we are forced to dwell in situations that stifle our happiness, only to learn that happiness is indeed a state of mind. Whether it is a hostile work environment, a toxic person in your circle of friends, an unfavorable living situation, a challenging course, a sour relationship or a cantankerous spirit, all have the potential to tear you down and take your joy if you allow it to. However, once you realize that you can choose happiness in the midst of what may appear to be a chaotic situation, then you will be able to walk through this life with a double dose of happiness.

Each day you awake is an opportunity for you to choose what frame of mind you want to operate in. You may have some mornings where the traffic is heavy, you get a run in your new pair of tights, the coffee machine breaks down disabling you from having that first cup of coffee, your kids may be fighting, your dog may have torn that favorite tie to shreds, birds may have pooped all over your car, your alarm may not have gone off, there may be subway delays, your flight may get canceled at the last minute, your spouse may totally tick you off right before you leave for work and the list goes on Gems. However, with all of life's little nuisances, one is still left with the opportunity to simply smile and shake it off!

There will often be an unexpected turn of events causing your very own plan to go straight out of the window. However, sometimes those tiny inconveniences are the very things we need in order to remind us that we are indeed human and very much alive. Sometimes the very thing we dread is the one thing that we need to give us that extra jolt. We may spring into an action or express an emotion that very well needed to be expressed, but because we subconsciously held things in without even knowing, we may have neglected to release those emotions sooner. Life serves as a teacher, healer, provider and sustainer. All of the wonderful things that we need as human beings, life affords through God's gracious hands. Life is tough enough as it is, you might as well smile through all of the disappointments and pain. I am not saying that it will always be easy to simply grin and bear it. However, if

THE PRECIOUS GEM COLLECTION

you at least try your best to give happiness the lead role, you will find that you cannot lose.

Emerge. Evolve. Transform. Transcend.

THE PRECIOUS GEM COLLECTION

PERSEVERANCE

With all the things that could go wrong in a day, the fact that you are still standing is an indication that something has gone right!

There may be times in life when you feel like you have lost the ultimate battle. You may have brought your A-game, put your best foot forward, and you may have given life all that you've got. However, somehow you still managed to come up short. You may have had to face extreme adversity in your life, overcome insurmountable odds and weather torrential storms. However, even the most tumultuous of times may be your ticket into your grandest blessing and long awaited miracle. Even with all of the obstacles that may be in your way, you are more than equipped to defeat every last one of them. There may be a ton of hindrances or stumbling blocks in your way in the form of people, places and things. However, not one thing can stop you unless you allow it to. Yeah, one might be thrown way off course at times and be caught between a rock and a hard place, but that's when creativity is truly born.

Have you ever found yourself at a place in your life where it seems as if you have reached a dead end or hit rock bottom? Did you feel that there was no place for you to turn? That is when you must look up, because up and out of the pit of sorrow is the only place you can go from there. Sometimes life will take you through valley experiences to wake you up and get your complete attention. Sometimes we get so caught up moving forward and staying strong that we totally miss the big picture. The valley experience is where lessons are learned, faith is renewed, strength is built, courage arises, hope is gained, love grows, genuine support is sought, peace is maintained, sanity is sustained and every wonderful part of you that needs to be groomed and further developed is refined like silver, enhancing your value. Sometimes we must go through the fire to come out like gold. The key to surviving any valley experience is perseverance. Life will sometimes deal you a low blow, one that could quite possibly knock you off of your feet,

THE PRECIOUS GEM COLLECTION

causing you to lose all balance, focus, and fervor. However, the first mistake we make when we are facing a challenge is choosing to stay down. We get so discouraged that we decide to give up, give in, throw in the towel and throw up our hands in defeat. We start to believe that all hope is lost, and instead of getting a tighter grip on faith, we latch right on to futility. We stop moving forward, when in reality this is the time when we need to run the race that is set before us with endurance and perseverance. There is always hope for a brighter tomorrow if we just make it through today. Take life one day at a time, one step at a time. Don't give up Gems! Give in to faith, love, peace, hope, and all of the joy that is due to each and every one of you. The race is not given to the swift, but to the one who can endure to the end.

The victory is yours Gems! Keep walking, keep running, keep fighting and most of all Precious Gems, keep the faith!

THE PRECIOUS GEM COLLECTION

WHAT IS A "HATER" REALLY?

What is a "HATER" really? Is it someone who genuinely despises you, or is it someone who truly admires you? However, because of their own insecurity, is it hard for them to show you some love or give you props, while their admiration for you translates into animosity and disdain?

This question leaves the floor open to many possibilities, as there is no one right answer set in stone. This is the point where your perception becomes your reality! I have made a couple of recent discoveries regarding life, love and the pursuit of happiness. For one, we live in a society where terminology is widespread and used interchangeably. For instance, the word "HATER" has become a universal term used to often describe someone who hates on another individual by throwing unnecessary shade and aiming their own self-imposed disdain at that individual. It usually occurs when someone who is unhappy with their own life or internal essence, so much so that they are willing to focus all of their negative energy and misery on someone else in an effort to keep the focus and energy off of themselves. What I have realized is that if someone hates on you for no apparent reason from the start, they must first love something about you, or see something in you that they aspire to be. On the other hand, they just may be filled with hatred for themselves and a natural contempt for anyone who crosses their path who appears to be doing "better," all of which lies at the root of envy, jealousy and misery. No one on God's green earth is exempt from the negative energy that is spewed from the heart of another. We have all at one time or another fallen prey to the insensitivity and insecurities of others. However, it is up to us to extinguish and demolish these negative forces with the power of love and light that resides within.

THE PRECIOUS GEM COLLECTION

What is the first thing that comes to your mind when you hear the word HATER? It is usually something negative right? Well Gems, if you really look beyond the surface and deeply into an individual that fits the description, you will find that the word used to describe them that naturally holds a negative connotation can also be looked at in a positive and reinforcing light. Your perception is your reality. How you see something is most often the way it is reflected in your life. I remember a time when I would just cry my eyes out trying to figure out why people in the world were so insensitive and cruel, but then one day it hit me! Call it an epiphany.

Well Gems, while I was exhausting every possibility, expending all of my positive energy trying to understand the mind of a "hater" and everything associated with their actions, I realized that I was wasting precious and valuable amounts of time and energy in the process. You see, once someone realizes that we all possess a light and a thirst for more in this life, life then turns into a huge competition for them. People no longer want to work together to achieve a greater good, nor do they want to see the next person succeed or get ahead, especially if it means that they will be left in what we call "the dust." This is when jealousy, envy, greed, hatred, and all too many other negative entities begin to grow and fester in the hearts of individuals. Instead of loving one's way to the top, one decides to take on the role of a "hater." It's almost like it's some sort of fetish or way of life now, it's like people are walking around saying "I am a hater and I'm proud of it!" It seems to be the "in" thing for some.

Well Gems, the reality is that one must either look up to you, or identify with something that you reflect or represent in order for them to hate on you, criticize you, bad mouth you or slander you. They are most often trying to get to a place within themselves where they can feel comfortable and secure. However, instead of allowing others the room to be themselves and fulfill their own destinies, a hater blocks and throws shade. When one gets to a place where the concerns and negative opinions of others don't really affect them or play too much on their psyche, that is when teaching, healing, and loving can begin.

You see Gems, in order to love others, one must first be able to love oneself. I will be the first to tell you that people will test you Gems, sometimes leaving you with little to no choice but to check their negativity. You may want to leave all character, poise, humility and grace behind at times, and you may even want to stoop to the same level of ignorance that others dwell on just to get your point across. However, is it really worth it Gems? Not at all! Don't you know that there is power in your tongue? Life and death resides in your words, so before you react, lash out in anger and lose your composure, please think it over and try your best to act out of love. The easiest thing to do is fight fire with fire, and the hardest thing to do is turn the other cheek. However, I guarantee you if you just take the time to see beyond the ignorance displayed, you will be a better person for it.

Life is your greatest teacher, and what does not kill you will in essence make you stronger. Rise above injustice, hatred, negativity and haughty contempt. Lead by example! Hold on to your dignity and put your pride aside. So many people are in need of love, and while you may be one person, we can all make a difference if we try. When people try to put a dimmer on and try to snuff out your light, simply light their fire by being that radiant light that you are. When you are yourself without reservation, you then give others permission to be exactly who they are. Give someone the gift of light and love by showing them some love in spite of their ignorance.

Love and live life Gems! You are loved Precious Gems and you are light!

THE PRECIOUS GEM COLLECTION

TRUTH

What is truth? Is it something that can be clearly defined? Do we all hold tightly to the same truths? Can the truth be partial or impartial? Is truth even truth? So many questions, and yet the answer remains the same. The truth is nothing but factual, correct, precise, valid, accurate, actual, authentic, bona fide, dependable, direct, exact, genuine, honest, undeniable and sincere. There are no ifs, ands, or buts about it! Whether it is tangible or abstract, there is not one part fiction involved in the truth. It is not counterfeit, pretended, fictitious, imaginary, misleading, beguiling, deceiving, delusive, dishonest, distorted, faulty, fraudulent, inaccurate, phony, trumped up or unreal.

For instance, what may be true for some people may not be true for most people. However, the bottom line is that it all still goes back to pure fact. Sometimes the hardest thing for someone to do is tell the whole truth and nothing but the truth. We have all heard the saying, "The truth hurts." Well, this statement may be true at times, but I guarantee you that the pain from the truth feels much better than the pain deceit can bring. Yet and still, it is still a topic that most refuse to deal with or can barely even handle.

We live in a world where knock-offs are accepted and genuine quality is most often rejected. Integrity and honesty are lacking. We are each human and imperfect, but the truth remains the same. One should strive to lead with truth, even if it means standing alone or walking away from people, places and things that are contrary to the truth. The easiest thing for one to do is to twist and bend the truth, especially when it's convenient. However, where does that really get you? NOWHERE!

If I had to count the many times I have had to be brutally honest with myself and others, even when I did not want to, I would lose count. It is not something that comes very easy to many people, but it really should be the easiest thing one grows to do. I have found that in my life, honesty is the only way to operate. There may even be times when the truth is challenged, but you must always remember what the truth is and hold firmly to it. Nobody

THE PRECIOUS GEM COLLECTION

can destroy the truth, because it is indestructible and it always bears witness to itself. I am not saying to be anal about it Gems, such as going around telling people exactly what's on your mind. You are still entitled to your own private thoughts and opinions. However, when faced with a situation that requires the truth, be sure to tell it straight from the heart. Even when you fall short, you can still allow the truth to come forth. You'll never lose, trust that!

Do your best to do unto others what you would have them do unto you. We are still human and each of us is still a work in progress. We are not called to be perfect, but if we can come as close to it as possible by simply walking in integrity and the fullness of who God created us to be, then the balance between imperfection and perfection can be met. In this day and age, you are almost seen as something extraterrestrial if you speak honestly and openly from the heart. However, I would encourage everyone under the sun to stand up for the truth, because at the end of the day it is you who has to answer to you, it is you who has to look in the mirror at yourself, it is you who has to wake up with yourself, it is you who truly defines who you are. I speak for myself not to impose my truth on you, but to challenge you to seek your own truth. We all know the difference between true and false, but it is what we do in the face of choosing between the two that truly makes all the difference in the world.

Live in truth. Love in truth. Seek the truth. Walk in truth. Be the truth!

THE PRECIOUS GEM COLLECTION

A MOTHER'S LOVE

     Giver of life. Nurturer. Caretaker. Provider. Protector. Beautiful. Compassionate. Strong. Loving. Committed. Faithful. Driven. Selfless. Humble. Willing. Capable. Noble. Virtuous.

Of all the words that can describe a mother's love, one word that best fits the description would have to be UNCONDITIONAL. Before you were even formed in the womb, you were a divine part of creation. When you were conceived you became a long awaited gift. As you developed day by day, week to week, and month to month, every part of her was a part of you, and she gave to you every part of her. Your arrival changed the world and the lives of those who waited for you to make an entrance. Above all, you changed the life of the woman who carried you for nine months. Her womb was your resting place as you nestled in a warm and nurturing place inside of her, tucked away in a secure place that you could call home for a while. You ate her laughter, and sometimes drunk from the cup of her sorrow. Every craving became your treat. Every toss and turn knocked you off of your feet. You were protected by her love. You were fashioned by God, fearfully and wonderfully made in His divine and beautiful image. She made the ultimate sacrifice, she gave you life. Her needs were no longer primary, they came second to yours. She never thought twice about providing all that you needed to get by. She would give an arm to ensure your survival, never allowing anyone or anything to bring you harm. If you couldn't sleep, she was up too, rocking away your tears. If you desired food to eat, she was light on her feet, always quick to make sure every need was met. Never would she place you in harm's way, she would give her life for you. You were a ray of light and you brightened up her days. You gave her strength, the kind of strength that only a child could bring. You taught her new things. Her life would never be the same. It was forever changed the day you were born. No one could ever take your place, nor could they replace all the love she has for you. You are her everything!

     Of all the gifts in the world that God could have granted me, my mother's love is the greatest of them all. When I was a child, I relied on my mother for everything, but I still did not understand to the fullest just how precious a mother's love truly was. When I became a teenager I fought tooth and nail to do things my way, while taking hold of the strength, courage, and wisdom that my mother displayed. Now that I am an adult, I realize more now than ever the magnitude of my mother's love. And, I understand the significance of the term "Mothers know best!" I have found that as I get older, my mother and I are a lot more alike than not. We share so many of the same qualities and ideas. I value and cherish her opinions more than I could have ever when I was yet a child. Her support is very much needed as my place as her child, and hers as my guardian will never change.

You see Gems, no matter how old you get, your mother will always be your mother. Yeah, there may be differences along the way, but the reality is that you only get one, and that one loves you more than you will ever know or understand. No matter who your caretaker is, biologically or not, the meaning behind the word mother truly goes deeper than just her being the woman who gave birth to you. She took care of you, she clothed you, and she fed you. She made sacrifice upon sacrifice to ensure your safety and security. We have all had people in our lives that may have taken on the role of a mother or caretaker in many ways. Let us not dare to forget about grandmothers, aunts, cousins, sisters or perhaps even friends. No matter who raised you, love is still love. So on this day, I give props to a woman who gave me the greatest gift of love.

Mommy's little angel for life! I love you mom.

THE PRECIOUS GEM COLLECTION

SEIZE THE DAY!

A new year. A new season. A new beginning. A brand new day!

A freshness that allows one a clean slate is a beautiful gift to behold. In addition, most often a newfound strength, courage, wisdom, faith, restored soul, hope and new perspective are all closely associated with this newness. While your yesterday may have been filled with thoughts of futility, and days of old may have been filled with fear and disappointment, don't despair. This is a new day, a time for you to begin again!

The canvas is empty. Yesterday is long gone. Live in the moment. Look ahead to the bright and wonderful things that await you. Far off in the distance there is a beautiful horizon calling out your name. Let it resonate with the song in your heart. Don't be afraid to respond. Shout it aloud! Let it resound like the roaring thunder for the entire world to hear. It's a new day! Seize every moment with fervor, and let your passion fly. Don't be afraid to try, all that you need to get by lives inside of you. Seize the day!

THE PRECIOUS GEM COLLECTION

DADDY'S LITTLE GIRL

As far back as I can remember, my dad and I have always been closer than close. He's my ace! When I look at photographs of me and him, we are just grinning from ear to ear. We were two peas in a pod. And let's not forget to mention that I look just like him. My dad also gave me my name. My mom often tells me stories of the day I was born. She said that my father was in the delivery room with her one minute, and the next moment he just shot out of the delivery room like a jumping jack, ran out of the hospital and down the street to his mother's house. My mom said he shouted out "She looks like me mom, she looks like me!" When I hear these stories I just smile.

It's a blessing to know that you are loved so unconditionally by another human being, and when you grow up, you can still remember things that touched your life as a child. I remember my dad taking me for walks at the New York Botanical Garden. He would talk to me like I was an adult and really listen to my response. My mom said that he would push my stroller with such pride, smiling to and from every destination. Every time I had an event, my dad would do everything in his power to attend. Whether I was singing at a talent show, graduating from high school, going off to college, you name it, he was there. And to this day, there is nothing that I need that he wouldn't give me. He gives me advice on careers, relationships, fashion, spirituality, writing, performing and everything pertaining to life in general. He taught me how to ride my bike, I was always too afraid to fall down or get dirty. He was always quick to my defense when someone hurt me. I will never ever forget the many times he dried my tears and told me "Baby girl, it's all going to be just fine. Love is the light!" I remember when I first moved to California by myself, my father was one of the first to visit. My father sheltered me so much growing up, sometimes to the point where I felt like I would never be able to function without his presence.

THE PRECIOUS GEM COLLECTION

He treated me like a princess, and he also set the tone for others to love, honor, and respect me. He taught me how to live
from within, encouraging me to never compromise or jeopardize who I am for anyone or anything. He shared knowledge and wisdom, knowing that one day his baby girl would have to go off and face the world on her own. We have had our share of differences, just like any father-daughter relationship. However, there is no one or nothing that could shake our love for each other or break our bond. No time or distance could ever separate us or sever our tie, distance is only geography.

Daddy's little girl for life! I love you dad.

THE PRECIOUS GEM COLLECTION

LIVE

Am I happy? Am I happy enough with myself and in my life? Can I let go?

If we can all answer these questions with a resounding "yes!", then our home going will not be a sorrowful event, instead, it will be a celebration of life. This talk of life and death is to get you to really take inventory on your days spent on this earth. This is a tough subject for most. Moreover, who really wants to discuss death and dying? It's rather depressing if you ask me, but it is a reality that we must all face. The point is that we must be careful that we don't spend most of our days living as someone who has nothing to live for. Life is a gift, and we have it abundantly every single day that we are granted breath of life.

"Am I happy?"- This is a powerful question for each of us roaming the earth, because it causes us to go deep, maybe deeper than what we're used to going at times. Every day that we wake up and step foot out of our dwellings, we are susceptible to all kinds of things. We take a chance on life every single day. A dear friend of mine recently told me that nothing in life is certain, and that all you can do is give each day your best. We are human beings and our days on earth are numbered. It's a stark reality! However, you must live your life to the fullest each day. Give it the best you've got Gems! Yes, I am well aware that life is not always a walk in the park. However, you will find that life is a huge playground awaiting your arrival. It is not how you start that makes the difference, it is how you finish that makes all the difference in the world. What you do with your life and all that it affords you is where true fulfillment dwells. You don't have to be a superstar, millionaire, or person extraordinaire in order to be happy. You have a heart, mind, body and soul that afford you much more than any amount of money could ever buy you. Fame, fortune and other material entities are all additions to your life. They are extra added benefits, but by no means necessary should they define you.

THE PRECIOUS GEM COLLECTION

Think of it like the benefit seasoning provides Gems, and what it does for food. It adds flavor, color and a special texture to some. Without it, food would still be food. However, it would just be in its original state, serving its purpose regardless. Now don't get it twisted Gems, material blessings are always a plus, but never should it outweigh the intangible benefits of love, joy, peace and prosperity.

Ask yourself today and be honest with yourself. Are you happy? If the answer is no, then you must do all that you can today to make it a "yes". We only get one chance at life on earth. I want us all to finish great! Tell that loved one or friend that you love them. Let go of the past. Live in the moment more. Let go of fear. Travel the world. Live out your dreams. Follow your heart. Let love lead.

I love you so very much Gems, and while time and distance separates us all, let us remain connected in spirit. Live!

THE PRECIOUS GEM COLLECTION

EXHORTATION

Exhortation allows one to carefully and consciously advise and serve others in love, by being sensitive, available, open, ready and willing to serve. When you are able to open yourself up to sincerely promote the growth and development of another human being, you are blessed with not only a gift, but also a lot of heart.

You see Gems, there will be times when others seek your counsel, but they are not always going to be willing to hear the truth. However, the truth spoken in love will always do the job. Whether the message conveyed is received right away or at a later date, it will still take residence in the hearts and minds of the individuals who sought the advice. It's like planting a seed, watering it, and watching it grow as it blossoms into the entity it is supposed to be as it lives out its intended purpose. Like anything in life, things take time, but it is up to us to plant the seed. You must be willing to face rejection and criticism. You will not always gain the approval of the recipient, as the givers' responsibility is not to please, but to ensure growth. Feelings may not always be able to be spared, for we know that feelings and emotions are fleeting. However, the love you show another that enables progress and development will never cease. Sometimes the hardest thing to do is sit back and watch someone you love suffer an ill. However, once you realize that most often the very essence of that ill only seeks to teach, prune, and purify, you will then be able to show the necessary support.

As an exhorter, it is your duty to encourage and inspire in the spirit of love. You must be careful not to be judgmental, apathetic, selfish, or too proud. You just never know whose life is riding on something as simple as a word of encouragement. You may have changed a multitude of lives by granting a tiny bit of inspiration. You may even think that people are not really listening to the words that come out of your mouth all too often, but you would be surprised. Never should we underestimate the power of the spoken word. There may also be times when you are called upon to simply listen and not speak.

THE PRECIOUS GEM COLLECTION

This is where the power of sensitivity comes into play. Sometimes we get so caught up in our own world that we forget that we are all human and we all hurt in some way. The common denominator between all human beings is the fact that we all have feelings. And, while some may be hurt easier than others, feelings are still feelings. So many people are walking around just praying, hoping, and wishing someone would reach out to them, and you never know Gems, it could be you who lights their fire. With an open mind, a willing heart and arms wide open, you can totally alter lives. It's not as difficult as it may seem, for it is usually the smallest thing that truly amounts to something great!

THE PRECIOUS GEM COLLECTION

IMPRESSIONS

I did something different today Gems. I took a different route home to get a change of scenery, and I did myself a great service by doing so. On my way home, I witnessed such a beautiful display of love that it really opened my eyes to something special. So often we get caught up in verbiage that we forget that the intention behind what we say and do has an even greater impact at times than what was actually said and done. It is not what we say, or what we do that leaves a lasting impression, the imprint is often left by the way we say the things we say, and the way we do the things we do.

Have you ever run into someone that you haven't seen for a while, didn't their eyes just light up upon seeing you? Did you feel good after saying something to someone knowing that the words you uttered came straight from your heart and your intentions were sincere? While verbal communication plays a huge part in the way we interact with people now of days, we must remember that the non-verbal is just as important. I am sure we have all heard the saying "The eyes are the window to the soul," or, "The eyes never lie." It's something I have found to be very true Gems! Figuratively speaking, it makes much sense because the eyes do play a big part in effective communicating. Have you ever looked into someone's eyes and saw sorrow even though they wore the biggest smile on their face? Have you ever had someone tell you something that sounded good, but it did not sit right with your spirit? It all goes right along with intentions, and the true intention behind everything said and done carries the greatest weight.

I rode the 8th Avenue Express train home this evening instead of taking my normal 6th Avenue route, and I witnessed an interaction between a father and son that truly brought a smile to my face. The son had to be about four or five years of age, and oh boy was he acting out in the worst way on the train. His unruly behavior not only drew attention to his father, but also to himself. While the father had every right to get upset or embarrassed by his son's behavior, he surely did a good job keeping it under control.

THE PRECIOUS GEM COLLECTION

He did not get all bent out of shape, nor did he lose his temper. He held his composure and kept his cool, he did not step one inch out of character. He appeased the situation by talking to his son in a firm yet loving tone. He talked to his son as if he was an adult on his level, and the response was utterly amazing. The father went on to saying that he would take his son's toys away until he got his act together and showed him some respect by listening to him. The young boy responded in a manner that was commendable as he said, "Daddy, I am going to listen to you now." He then took his seat and sat upright until my stop came at 145th street, and mind you, this episode started at Canal Street, approximately 25 to 30 minutes earlier. I was so moved by the way the father handled the situation, and even more impressed by the way the son responded. It just goes to show you that effective communication does not mean displaying loud and boisterous tones, obscene behavior, or even losing all composure to get a point across. One does not have to get out of character or totally stoop to a lower level; all that does is add fuel to the fire. Love covers a multitude of entities, one of which is discipline. Moreover, even as it graces numerous arenas, it never loses its inherent power. Love is love.

THE PRECIOUS GEM COLLECTION

LET THE SILENCE BE BROKEN

Every day, someone somewhere wakes up to a nightmare. And, every night, someone somewhere falls asleep hoping to never have to be a part of one. It is so heavy on my heart right now to speak life into other human beings who might otherwise be bound by fear and who may never find out that they can be liberated in mind, body, and soul. This goes out to the young and the old. This goes out to the men and women out there who have been scarred, and who cannot seem to free their minds in order to free their souls. This goes out to all of you individuals out there in the world who have broken the silence. Your courage is exemplary! If you as an individual know someone who is facing a tumultuous time, take them by the hand, look them square in the eye, and say "No more shall you be bound, you are set free!"

Sometimes all one needs is a word of encouragement to push them in the right direction, a pat on the back to let them know that they are doing just fine, a hand to hold to let them know that they are not alone, and blessed assurance to help them heal and move forward. Not for one moment do I ever want anyone under the sound of my voice or a recipient of these inspirations to feel alone, lost or broken. For as surely as God is the author and finisher of my faith, I will stand in the gap via inspiration, prayer, support, etc. We only get one life, may we each use it to accelerate our humanity in some way, shape or form.

So many people are carrying weights that only seek to pull them under and hold them down. There are things that have happened in your past that have plagued you day in and day out, and you do not know where to begin to even tell it. You are afraid of the freedom and rejection that comes along with the silence being broken. Whether it is your spirit that has been broken to the point of no return, your manhood or womanhood robbed, youth stolen, joy taken, peace diminished or faith lost, it is time to let the silence be broken. For it is only in breaking the silence and speaking the truth that healing can truly begin!

THE PRECIOUS GEM COLLECTION

Speak up and speak out against the injustice that has been done to you. You do not have to carry those burdens anymore, the chains are broken, and you are no longer bound by pain, betrayal or deceit. Release horrible memories and break free! You've been told that it's not easy to let go of the things that have tormented you for so long, you have been told that healing is impossible, and you have been sentenced to a lifetime of pain and misery because somewhere, somehow, you were lied to. Don't listen to the lies that say you will never be better, see better or do better. They are lies, and it's time to speak life!

Listen up my sister! Listen up my brother! You are not alone. You are a child of God, wise, guided and loved. You no longer have to swim in sorrow, nobody can hurt you anymore. You are worthy of love and you are a winner. Stop blaming yourself for the wrong done to you. It is not your fault! Stop being a victim of someone else's insensitivity, malady and ignorance. It stops here! I am praying for each and every one of you, known and unknown. I am holding your hand and supporting you through the healing process. I am loving you through every change. I am in support of your courageous stance. You are victorious this day, and you shall be victorious every single day hereafter. Live your life unencumbered and unfettered by restraints. Begin again and start today! The future is even bigger, brighter, and better than yesterday.

There might be one person out there that needs to know that their heart is felt or heard amidst the noisome atmosphere of the world. With that said Gems, I want to encourage each of you to follow your heart and listen to the spirit within. Sometimes you will be moved to do or say things that in the natural realm seem outrageous or irrational. However, I can attest to the reaffirming power of the spoken word. If there is one thing that we have in this life that is a valuable tool and a positive reinforcement, it is our voice. We hold the power to positively change lives, and you just don't know whose life you may have changed or will change by speaking up. Listen to your heart and follow through.

THE PRECIOUS GEM COLLECTION

There is someone out there who needs to hear exactly what your heart is moving you to say or do.

THE PRECIOUS GEM COLLECTION

TO BE A KID AGAIN

This past weekend I went to visit one of my best friends in New Paltz and we had a blast! The kind of blast I am talking about Gems, is the kind where you are care-free, stress-free and work-free. I needed time to clear my head of all the clutter, and the hustle and bustle of the Big Apple was not going to cut it for me this time. I had to go on a mini escape, and it did wonders for my soul. I did something this weekend that I have not done in a long, long time. I went to a playground and got on the swings. Talk about a high that I did not want to come down from. I almost cried because I realized something very profound. I came to the realization that somewhere on the way up from childhood, through adolescence and up into adulthood, I lost a tiny bit of my youth. When we are children, we tend to be in a hurry to get old, and when we become adults and have to deal with adult responsibilities, we desire our youth.

There is nothing like the innocence of a child. Children are so pure and untainted in a lot of ways. They live free and unencumbered lives. They are unfettered by restraints, unmoved and undistracted by the pangs of life. One can be so busy that they forget how to be a kid again, and a youthful spirit is something we must fight to maintain. Youthful exuberance is a gift, if only we would take hold of it more often. It is okay to let our hair down and exhale from time to time. It is okay to run around in a field and roll around in the grass. It is okay to eat ice cream cones and sit down for a glass of milk and cookies with friends. It is okay to run along a path and kick rocks. It is okay to play in the sand. It is okay to dream like a child and believe for things deemed impossible by society. It is okay to laugh and color outside of the lines. It is okay play on the seesaw. It is okay to jump rope. It is okay to rollerblade, ride a bike, and play catch. It is okay to play hide & go seek. It is okay to climb the highest mountain and swim the deepest sea. It is okay to go horseback riding and scuba diving. It is okay to do all of the things that make you happy. It is okay to experience that childlike fervor that keeps you in a place of ceaseless dreaming. We often forget to nurture our inner child.

Emerge. Evolve. Transform. Transcend.

THE PRECIOUS GEM COLLECTION

There is a little girl/ little boy on the inside of each of us that yearns to be acknowledged.

Do you ever notice that children are not as stressed as adults because they take the time to play? Do you ever notice that kids are not as hung up on themselves because innately they know that it is okay to fall down? Do you ever notice how kids don't mind getting dirty because they know that dirt is not permanent? Do you ever notice the smile on a child's face when they are playing a game with their friends? Children possess a gift that just keeps on giving, a youthful spirit that thrives on joy and laughter. We all need to take a trip to the fountain of youth every once in a while. Whether your fountain is a playground, empty canvas, football field, basketball, court, baseball field, race track, horse stable, swimming pool, beach, recording studio, kitchen, bookstore, movie theatre, garden, zoo, classroom, dance studio, shopping mall or Hawaii, make it your business to revisit the place where the child in you can run free, even if it is only for a moment!

THE PRECIOUS GEM COLLECTION

GO TO YOUR DESTINY!

We each have a divine purpose to fulfill on this earth, and there is NOTHING that can stop you from reaching your destiny. We all possess gifts that are unique and special, and if we look within ourselves, we will be able to locate our purpose. Everything that we need to get through in this life is on the inside: FAITH, PEACE, LOVE, JOY, STRENGTH, COURAGE and WISDOM. Even when obstacles get in the way, they are a major part of the plan for fulfilling your purpose and reaching your destiny.

Have you ever applied for a job that you really wanted and you did not get it, but another opportunity came your way that was even better? Have you ever wanted to move and something would always deter you, but someone came into your life that you would not have met if you moved? Have you ever wanted to take a vacation and were not able to take time off from work, but later you won a free trip to the same destination that you desired? Have you ever lost a loved one and thought that life could not possibly go on without them, but a baby was born into your family shortly after that person passed? Have you ever been in a relationship and thought that the person you were with was right for you and things did not work out, but after you moved on, someone special came into your life that was perfect for you? Have you ever had a vision for your life so big that caused folk to think that you had lost your mind? In turn, did you lose some friends in the midst of carrying out your dream, but you decided to chase your dream anyway, and by some miracle a way was made and your dream was fulfilled?

These are all prime examples of preparation for the best that is in store for you. I am here to tell you that there is an open door waiting for you to walk through it. Do not be discouraged when things do not go the way you planned, I guarantee you that something better is on the way. There were so many times in my life when I wanted things so bad, but I could not obtain them on my time or I simply did not obtain them at all.

Emerge. Evolve. Transform. Transcend.

THE PRECIOUS GEM COLLECTION

I would fuss and kick up my heels in a frenzy, only to realize in the end that what I wanted was not what I really needed, but what I really needed turned out to be what I really wanted. All
I have to say is that life is full of surprises, and the road always curves when you least expect it. There are so many beautiful things in store for you, and I want you to never forget that nothing or nobody can stop what God has for you. Go To Your Destiny!

THE PRECIOUS GEM COLLECTION

ONE CHAPTER ENDS

A NEW ONE BEGINS...

Most Dear & Precious of Gems,

I thank God for the opportunity to share the abundance of my heart and journey of my soul with you Precious Gems. I hope that the instrument played a fine tune that has blessed you, and will continue to bless you eternally. May each inspiration live on through each and every, single one of your beautiful souls.

I would like to thank you Precious Gems for accompanying me on this journey. As you continue to walk down this path of life, may you continue to emerge, evolve, transform and transcend the ills of this world as you walk in the fullness of who you were created to be and walk out your divine purpose. As I turn the page and embark on a new journey of inspiration, I want to take the time to extend my heartfelt gratitude for all of your support, love, prayers, and well wishes. We have walked this road of inspiration together, and while the ending of one chapter does mark the beginning of a new one, I want you all to hold tightly to those things that will never cease. While each day brings forth something new and different, love never ceases. The transforming power of God's love changes people, and it most certainly changes things. It has been wonderful sharing my heart and soul with you.

The journey has been amazing, and it only gets better. May you take the words that I have given you and write them in your hearts. Hold them close, as they will always serve as a reminder that we are connected heart-to heart, spirit-to-spirit. As you move forward on this journey, may love rest at the center of all that you think, say and do. Love yourself and be good to others. Give, and it shall be given unto you Precious Gems, in good measure, pressed down, shaken together and running over shall men give unto your bosom(Luke 6:38 KJV). For with the measure you use to give, it will be measured back to you. Let love rule in your hearts Gems. Smile in the face of adversity. Think positively and positivity follow.

THE PRECIOUS GEM COLLECTION

So Gems, as I prepare for the next phase of my inspirational journey, my hope and prayer is that you will also turn the page. Turn the page on a new chapter of your life with each new day that you are granted. May the road curve to meet your every expectation as you tread down this path of life, and may you forever be blessed. Always remember that this is not the end, but rather the beginning of something beautiful and new. Fly high on the wings of faith, you are empowered to prosper!

Go to your destiny… The Best Is Yet To Come!

Love & Light,
Ajá

THE PRECIOUS GEM COLLECTION

LET US PRAY

"Our Father which art in heaven,

Hallowed be thy name.

Thy kingdom come,

Thy will be done in earth,

as it is in heaven.

Give us this day our daily bread.

And forgive us our debts,

as we forgive our debtors.

And lead us not into temptation,

but deliver us from evil:

For thine is the kingdom,

and the power,

and the glory,

forever.

Amen."

~Matthew 6:9-13

May the Lord meet you right where you are; He is omnipresent, omnipotent and omniscient. Keep the faith Precious Gems; the victory is yours both now and forevermore.

Emerge. Evolve. Transform. Transcend.

THE PRECIOUS GEM COLLECTION

CELEBRATE LIFE

"In life, we are faced with many challenges, and these challenges are placed in our path to build strength and character. However, while they may seek to jade our focus, kill our dreams, dismiss our hope, cloud our visions, and steal our joy, we must not succumb."

"Impossible is an illusion, for the unlimited potential and power within each of us is immeasurable."

Emerge. Evolve. Transform. Transcend. Soar…

~Ajá Marie Grant, C.C.

THE PRECIOUS GEM COLLECTION

AN INVITATION FOR YOU

As noted in the Word of God (John 10:10), "The thief comes only to steal and kill and destroy; I came (Christ) that they may have life, and have it abundantly.

Do you desire to experience that abundant life in Christ? If so, I would like to invite you to make Christ the Lord and Saviour of your life, for it is with your heart that you believe and are justified, and it is with your mouth that you confess and are saved. (Romans 10:10)

PRAYER OF SALVATION:

"Lord, I'm asking you to come into my life. I need you, please forgive me of my sins. Deliver me and set me free from the lie of the enemy. I believe what the Bible says in Romans 10: 9-11, and I confess with my mouth that Jesus is Lord, and I believe in my heart that God raised him from the dead. Save me, I pray this in the name of Almighty Jesus. Amen.

AN INVITATION FOR PRAYER:

If there be anyone, man, woman, or child who is in need of prayer, who has an urgent prayer request, or who would like to share a report of praise, please feel free to send them, and I will make it my business to pray and stand in the gap for you. It is by the grace of almighty God that I am able to get up and do this each day, as I am merely a vessel and an instrument of His love and grace. May this instrument be used for His glory always. You may send your prayer requests and/or praise reports to Zoesoleil@yahoo.com.
All prayer requests will be kept confidential.

Have a beautiful and blessed existence!
The Best Is Yet To Come!

Love & Light,
Ajá

Emerge. Evolve. Transform. Transcend.

THE PRECIOUS GEM COLLECTION

ABOUT THE AUTHOR

Ajá Marie Grant, C.C., is a lifestyle and sports coach certified by the Life Coach Institute of Orange County. In 2008 she founded Zoë Soleil (www.ZoeSoleil.com), a pioneering and innovative firm designed to support the elevation of humanity, by equipping individuals of all ages with the tools necessary to create a balanced lifestyle and live a life unfettered by restraints.

Additionally, as an alumna of Fordham University, Ajá is heavily steeped in the tradition of excellence, as Fordham University's long-standing commitment to the realization of prudence and the dissemination of knowledge through research and the highest quality of education has prepared her for leadership roles in a variety of industries worldwide.

The career she has built in a variety of diverse roles and industries has afforded her the opportunity to not only be an administrator, but also a gatekeeper, mentor, advisor, consumer advocate, event specialist and industry liaison. She has had the great fortune of wearing many hats. Moreover, she has forged invaluable relationships that have enabled her to gain valuable knowledge and experience. She has not only received insight into how various organizations are run and maintained, but also how leadership truly does play a major role in the efficiency of an operational group.

Through the diversity of her experiences Ajá became enthralled by sports, and as an administrative professional, visionary, and sports enthusiast with over 15 years of experience, her diverse skills and qualifications will enable her to be an asset to the lives and institutions of others. Sports has not only become a

THE PRECIOUS GEM COLLECTION

way for her to speak the language of the many sports aficionados in our society, but also a way for her to contribute to society as a whole, as she has found that sports is just as much about loyalty, leadership, teamwork, accessibility, endurance and motivation as it is about a team, a league, a game or a lucrative venture. Sports reach people on so many levels, and she has seen it firsthand not only as an active participant in society, but most importantly, in her work as a dedicated Life Coach.

Ajá has since obtained her Master of Science in Sports Business from New York University, where she was provided a place and opportunity to not only pursue her education and passion, but also gain personal achievement and professional development. Moving forward, you can expect to see Ajá tirelessly inspiring and touching the lives of others all over the world, as she is walking in the fullness of her purpose and in full pursuit of her destiny.

THE PRECIOUS GEM COLLECTION

CONTACT

AUTHOR: Ajá Marie Grant
WEBSITE: www.ZoeSoleil.com
EMAIL: Zoesoleil@yahoo.com

Visit Ajá at **http://www.zoesoleil.com/the_circle** for the latest inspirations, information on products and services, upcoming events, bulletins, blogs, photos, and more.

To receive a free e-mail newsletter delivering updates and inspiration, register directly by sending Ajá an e-mail to **Zoesoleil@yahoo.com**

To book Ajá for speaking engagements or literary work for hire, please send an email to **Zoesoleil@yahoo.com**

www.ingramcontent.com/pod-product-compliance
Lightning Source LLC
Chambersburg PA
CBHW050800160426
43192CB00010B/1588